JESUS
Friend and Savior

JESUS
Friend and Savior

Michael Pennock
and
James Hogan

AVE MARIA PRESS
Notre Dame, Indiana 46556

Excerpts from THE NEW JERUSALEM BIBLE, copyright © 1985 by Darton, Longman & Todd, Ltd. and Doubleday & Company, Inc. Reprinted by permission of the publisher.

© 1990 by Ave Maria Press, Notre Dame, IN 46556

International Standard Book Number: 0-87793-421-5

Cover photograph by Steve Moriarty

Text design by Katherine Robinson Coleman

Printed and bound in the United States of America.

Contents

		Introduction	7
Chapter	1	Jesus: Who Is This Person?	20
Chapter	2	Jesus: The Early Years	31
Chapter	3	Jesus Begins His Ministry	43
Chapter	4	Jesus and His People	53
Chapter	5	Jesus: The Teacher	64
Chapter	6	Jesus: A Gospel Portrait	78
Chapter	7	Jesus: A Personal Portrait	89
Chapter	8	The Paschal Mystery of Jesus: Passion, Death and Resurrection	101
Chapter	9	Belief Through the Ages	112
Chapter	10	Meeting the Risen Lord	124
		Tear-Out Section	137

■ *introduction* ■

Thank you for selecting *Jesus: Friend and Savior* to use with your students. We hope you will find the text helpful in proclaiming and reflecting on Jesus, the Lord. Through you and through their personal prayer and study, may your students discover the essential truth of the gospel: They are loved.

This introduction to the Teacher's Manual includes:

■ some preliminary remarks about Jesus as the focus of catechesis

■ an overview of the student text and how it fits into the series

■ the curriculum model used in both the student text and the Teacher's Manual

■ the format of this manual

Some Preliminary Remarks

Jesus is at the heart of our catechetical and religious education programs, both in high schools and parish programs. We don't overstate the case when we say that he is our reason for institutional existence. Thus, a Christology course should play a prominent role in our overall curriculum design.

Students today are searching for direction and meaning in their young lives. So many things vie for their attention: power, prettiness, prestige, possessions, popularity and sexual prowess. Students end up frustrated and unhappy when they pursue these things for their own sakes.

As catechists and religious educators, we have something of incalculable value to offer them: the joy of the gospel. This word of salvation centers on the person of Jesus Christ. He calls each of us and our students into friendship with him and leads us on "the way, and the truth, and the life" (Jn 14:6).

Both the National Catechetical Directory and Pope John Paul II's Apostolic Letter *Catechesi Tradendae* call for Christocentricity in catechesis. This means many things:

■ Jesus is the center of our teaching endeavors. "Everything else is taught in reference to him—and it is Christ alone who teaches" (*Catechesi Tradendae*, No. 6).

- The focus of teaching is not a body of abstract truths. Rather, its aim is the communication of the living God as revealed to us in Christ Jesus.

- Catechesis on Jesus will "draw its content from the living source of the word of God transmitted in Tradition and the Scriptures" (*Catechesi Tradendae*, No. 27).

- For our teaching to be effective and authentic, we catechists must be fully committed to Jesus Christ.

> Faith must be shared with conviction, joy, love, enthusiasm, and hope. "The summit and center of catechetical formation lies in an aptitude and ability to communicate the Gospel message." This is possible only when the catechist believes in the gospel and its power to transform lives. To give witness to the gospel, the catechist must establish a living, ever-deepening relationship with the Lord. He or she must be a person of prayer . . . (*Sharing the Light of Faith*, No. 207).

In a course devoted to Jesus, obviously we will have no difficulty fulfilling the requirement of "Christocentrism in catechesis." The other three points above remind us that we teach Jesus, not ourselves. To do this effectively and authentically we must draw on church teaching and scripture. However, no teaching about Jesus will ring true with students unless we are in love with the Lord who has called us to proclaim his message. Our commission is to share our faith to help enliven and strengthen the faith of our students. We have been invited into a personal relationship with a living Lord. As catechists we have accepted this gift and—in the name of the church—share with our students Jesus' invitation to a fuller life. Our goal includes both *knowledge about* and *knowledge of* Jesus.

Overview

Official catechetical documents, research on the religious concerns of young people,[1] the experience of colleagues and the author's experience of almost 25 years in the high school classroom have underscored the need to stress certain themes throughout the student text. They include the following:

- *Students need to hear that they are loved.* Both research and personal experience working with teens prove that Strommen's apt "cry of self-hatred" still applies to many of our students. Michael Warren reminds us that the media and those selling commodities (including music) exploit the adolescent subculture. Much of this exploitation sells the message of conditional love. An increasing number of our students come from single-parent homes. They often feel isolated and torn apart.

---

[1] See, for example, the following: Merton P. Strommen, *Five Cries of Youth*, New and Revised Edition (San Francisco: Harper & Row, Publishers, 1988), Charles M. Shelton, S.J., *Adolescent Spirituality* (Chicago: Loyola University Press, 1983, especially Chapter 4), Marisa Crawford and Graham Rossiter, *Religious Education in a Time of Rapid Change* (Sydney, Australia: Christian Brothers Province Resource Group, 1988, Chapter 1), and *Religious Education Journal*, Volume 81 (Spring 1986, dealing with the topic "Adolescence"). We'd also like to recommend Chapter 3 of Thomas M. Martin's *What Should I Teach?* (New York: Paulist Press, 1988) which shows some contemporary tensions, both in the church and in the personal theology of teachers, which catechists must consider when teaching Jesus.

As catechists, we can't solve all the problems of youth and certainly cannot reach all the students in front of us, some of whom are alienated from religion or find it boring or irrelevant. But what we can do is offer the person and message of Jesus. The news of Jesus is incredibly good news.

The gospel of Jesus is a genuine alternative to today's culture. Jesus joyfully tells of our dignity and worth. He invites us to a personal relationship with him, one that can transform our lives, giving them meaning and direction. Pope John Paul II states it well in speaking of providing a genuine faith education for adolescents:

> The revelation of Jesus Christ as friend, guide and model, capable of being admired but also imitated; the revelation of his message which provides an answer to the fundamental questions; the revelation of the loving plan of Christ the Saviour as the incarnation of the only authentic love and as the possibility of uniting the human race. . . (*Catechesi Tradendae*, No. 38).

The text attempts to present an authentic Jesus. This Jesus lives in his biblical word, the church, the sacraments and the students themselves who can get in touch with the Lord through personal prayer.

- *Students need to know that the Lord calls them personally. He needs them.* Much high school religious education presumes some pre-evangelization and much evangelization. Many of our students have not heard—or were not ready to hear—the gospel of the Lord. So we need to take time to review the basics, to proclaim Jesus to them (for example, through media, faith testimonials, Bible reading and enthusiastic lecturing) and to correct mistaken notions about Jesus and church teaching on him. But we reach a point where some genuine catechesis—an enriching and deepening reflection on what is proclaimed—can take place.

    Central to this catechetical effort is Jesus' call to faith. Jesus comforts those who are upset, but he also upsets the comfortable. Jesus' message of love and salvation demands response—faith and action. As sharers of the gospel, we must also challenge our students to be and do more. Jesus reminded us that faith without action is empty and does not guarantee salvation.

- *Students are in school to learn.* As teachers, we need not apologize for challenging our students intellectually. Part of the catechetical task is to enhance and enrich our students' faith knowledge. As educators, we do them a disservice by not sharing with them historical, theological, psychological, philosophical and other insights.

    Minimally, we can expect students to know the basics about Jesus: for example, his teachings, his miracles, the passion narrative, gospel theologies about him and church teaching through the ages. Ideally, though, we want to challenge students to make learning about Jesus a lifelong task. In teaching the content, we want to leave students with the impression that there is so much more to know and learn about Jesus. In showing them ways to pray to the Lord, we want them to sense that ending a course on Jesus is just the beginning of a lifelong journey with him.

- *Jesus calls for change.* In presenting Jesus, we must not so focus on the cognitive domain that we neglect the affective and behavioral dimensions of our students. Jesus' message about the kingdom requires *metanoia* or repentance. To this end, the text incorporates exercises, prayer reflections, activities and discussions that involve the whole person. In addition to knowing basic content, the text encourages students to discover, develop, respond, compare and contrast, pursue, identify, celebrate, feel, pray, live, proclaim, show concern and discuss what they learn.

■ *Jesus can be met in the Catholic community.* God's grace reaches all people. However, as Catholic teachers working in Catholic institutions, we need not apologize for presenting our belief that Jesus founded the church and lives on in it and works through it. The text, though respecting the beliefs of non-Christians and non-Catholics, draws on the Catholic tradition to present Jesus: its official teachings, sound theological reflection and the faith and sacramental life of Catholics through the centuries.

Features of the Text and Series

We would like to call to your attention some of the features of this text and the whole series.

Introduction. The introductory material includes:

1. A quote from the Bible that relates to one of the major themes of the chapter. *Sharing the Light of Faith* (#60a) reminds us that the Bible is a rich source of catechesis, and these texts draw liberally on scripture to relate themes to God's word.

2. A down-to-earth story or short anecdote as an attention "grabber" that also shows students how the topic relates to life.

3. An introductory exercise that requires values clarification or self-reflection. These exercises prepare students for the content of the chapter and stimulate interest in the topic.

Journal Entries. Sprinkled throughout the chapters are suggestions for topical entries in student journals that ask the students to apply the previous material to his or her personal life. They can usually be given as homework assignments. Keeping a journal in religious education offers many benefits such as:

■ encouraging self-reflection;

■ providing a meaningful way to pray;

■ helping apply, analyze, synthesize and evaluate what they learn;

■ developing and honing writing skills;

■ giving students a sense of pride and ownership in the course.

Journal-keeping in a course on Jesus has the additional benefit of encouraging a lifelong dialogue with Jesus. By re-reading their journals, students can evaluate their growing relationship with the Lord.

Each chapter ends with several journal assignments. One is a list of vocabulary words introduced in the chapter that may be unfamiliar to your students. Students are asked to keep a separate section in their journal notebooks where they can write the definitions of these words from a good dictionary. In this way, your students can build their vocabularies, another study skill your religion course can reinforce.

Exercises and Focus Questions. Throughout the chapter you will find several exercises or discussion questions that help break up the text and encourage students to reflect on what they are learning.

You will especially find many scripture-reading exercises in this text on Jesus. St. Jerome so well pointed out that ignorance of scripture is ignorance of Christ. Catechists must encourage scripture-reading as an authentic source of knowledge and intimacy with the Lord.

At the end of the chapter, the focus questions are targeted to student mastery of the cognitive content of the chapter. When key theological terms are introduced in the chapter, this section of the chapter identifies them. A glossary of selected theological terms included at the end of the text will help develop a common religious vocabulary for your students.

Prayer. An underlying theme of the text and the entire series is helping students learn how to pray. The Jesus text does this in the following ways:

■ Some journal entries require meditation, prayerful dialogue or reflection.

■ Some traditional prayers are included, for example, the shema, the Jesus Prayer, the "Seven Last Words of Jesus," Jesus' great priestly prayer at the Last Supper, the Magnificat and, of course, the Lord's Prayer. It is most appropriate to memorize, study and discuss these particular prayers in a course on Jesus.

■ Each chapter ends with a prayer reflection that sometimes includes a short teaching on prayer. It always includes a reflection and a resolution that calls for action that reinforces the theme of service.

■ Jesus is presented as a model pray-er. Both Jesus' personal example and his explicit teaching on prayer provide inspiration to students for becoming faithful persons of prayer in imitation of their Lord.

The entire series aims at a good and varied catechesis on prayer. Rather than treating prayer as "just another course," the series incorporates prayer as a critical theme in a holistic religious education.

Christian Lifestyle—Service. A fundamental theme of the text is service. The present text integrates this theme in the following ways:

■ Jesus is frequently presented as a model of service. His healing and teaching ministries, his explicit teaching on love and service (for example, in the Beatitudes) and his sacrifice on the cross are often cited to stress the students' need to imitate Jesus' actions and obey his words.

■ Several key exercises ask students to examine their gifts and commit themselves to use them in the service of others.

■ The connection between faith and service is explained.

■ Several individual and class "mini"-service projects are suggested.

■ A major section of one chapter focuses on Jesus' presence in others and our need to respond to them. An important activity is suggested to help students put their faith into action.

Curriculum Plan of the Text

A major assumption of the text is that you—the teacher—are primarily teaching students. The text is a tool to focus student attention and to help you attain your objectives for the course. A text stimulates student thought and reflection. It is only one element—albeit an important one—in your repertoire of resources for teaching students.

The objectives of your religious education program should determine the curriculum you teach. Ideally each religious education department develops and publishes its objectives for the four-year program which give a systematic catechesis. A good high school program achieves this by accomplishing these goals:

(1) teaching the Christian **message** as it is handed down in the Catholic tradition;

(2) fostering **Christian community**;

(3) developing student skills in **serving** others;

(4) helping students appreciate the celebration of Christian identity through **liturgy**.

We in high school religious education draw on a number of sources to develop the objectives of our four-year programs. For example, the *General Catechetical Directory*, *Sharing the Light of Faith*, *Catechesi Tradendae*, *To Teach as Jesus Did*, directives from the local bishop and diocesan religious education office and other pertinent documents are a rich resource for formulating objectives.

In addition, research findings on adolescent growth and development, needs analyses with our own students, practical classroom experience, the charism and spirituality of the religious orders that staff our schools and parent surveys all help religious educators put together a solid, yet timely and interesting program for students.

To improve our religious education programs we must periodically evaluate our objectives since they guide the curriculum. Objectives adopted for certain courses dictate the specific content to be taught, its scope, sequence and organization. They guide us in selecting the specific day-to-day methods and media we employ to teach our classes. They help us resist fads and control the overall direction of our course and programs.

The curriculum model suggested for this course relies heavily on periodic evaluation to help us verify how effectively we are accomplishing our goals. Evaluation helps us judge the suitability of the scope of our coverage, adjust our sequencing of the material and verify the reliability of our methods and choice of media to accomplish our goals. Evaluation might show us that some goals we set for ourselves are not achievable or may not be worth the time we spend on them.

Evaluation takes many forms. Quizzes and tests tell us how well we communicate to our students; professional colleagues from other institutions help us discover any lacunae in our programs; parent and student surveys tell us how well we meet their needs.

The text subscribes to a simple model of curriculum development sometimes known as a systems analysis approach or the "closed-loop" system. In schematic form it looks like this:

O B J E C T I V E S	Content
	Scope
	Sequence and Content Organization
	Method
	Media
	Evaluation

Objectives

Each chapter in this Teacher's Manual lists several objectives for the corresponding chapter of the student text. The following *general* objectives helped the author select and organize the content of the text.

That students . . .

1. *Reflect* on and *answer personally* Jesus' timeless question: "Who do you say that I am?"

2. *Know* some of the proofs for the existence of the historical Jesus and *explain* the continuity between "the Jesus of history" and the "Christ of faith."

3. *Characterize* various beliefs people have had about Jesus through the ages: his contemporaries, the Christian community through the centuries and opinions about Jesus today.

4. *Confront* the Jesus of the scripture, *discuss* a gospel portrait of Jesus and *characterize* in personal terms what this person means to them.

5. *Know* and *explain* a chronology of Jesus' life, focusing on his roles of healer, miracle-worker and teacher.

6. *Reflect on* and *respond to* Jesus' call to personal friendship with him.

7. *Understand* the various historical, religious, cultural, social and political forces that helped shape Jesus and the New Testament world.

8. *Hear, understand and discuss* the message of Jesus, especially the components of unconditional love, forgiveness, conversion, faith and response in service.

9. *Articulate* a personal portrait of Jesus.

10. *Experience* various ways of developing a personal relationship to Jesus Christ: for example, prayer, sacraments, service to neighbor.

11. *Explain, appreciate* and *apply* the paschal mystery to everyday life.

12. *Reflect on* and *discuss* the meaning of Jesus through his *titles* (e.g., Lord, Christ, Son of Man, Son of God, Word of God) and *roles* (e.g., teacher, model of prayer, savior, brother, friend).

13. *Know* and *explain* the various dogmatic teachings concerning Jesus.

14. In a personal way, *reflect on* their growing relationship with the Lord, especially through journal-writing and meeting him in others.

The text's goal is to develop content in a way that students will grow closer to Jesus. The goal of all catechesis is that more fruitful Christian living will proceed from knowledge of the Lord. We hope knowledge of the Lord will result in a more intense prayer life and a more active commitment to serve others.

As you develop your course objectives you will find *Sharing the Light of Faith*, Nos. 87-91, most helpful. These paragraphs list the principal elements of the Christian message as they deal with Jesus.

Content and Scope

The content of the course takes up topics you would expect to find in a high school Christology course—the history of Jesus' people, the events of Jesus' life, the main elements of his teaching, the paschal mystery, teaching and beliefs about him through the ages, his meaning for today. The scope is broad but it attempts to use specific examples to relate general ideas to the lives of the students.

No apology is made for giving some basic information and expecting students to master it. But the focus is not student memorization of unrelated facts. Above all, the book asks students to reflect on the *meaning* of what they are learning and judge the *relevance* of Jesus to their personal lives. The book tries to provide an answer to the question "Who do people say that I am?" Moreover, it returns often to the corollary "Who do *you* say that I am?"

Texts are geared primarily to the cognitive domain. This domain focuses on acquiring knowledge, gaining understanding, comprehending new knowledge and applying, analyzing, synthesizing and evaluating what is learned. *Jesus: Friend and Savior* fits this mold, but it also consciously appeals to the *behavioral* and *affective* domains of learning as well. Students need to *experience* the good news of Jesus, *rejoice* and *respond* to it and *actively live* it. Thus, values exercises, discussion questions, journal reflections, prayer experiences, scripture-reading activities and service projects are included in the text.

Sequence and Content Organization

Chapter One: Jesus: Who Is This Person?

1. "Who Do You Say I Am?"
2. Did Jesus Exist?
3. Jesus and His Contemporaries
4. Jesus: Some Modern Views

Chapter Two: Jesus: The Early Years

1. You Are Gift!
2. The Infancy Narratives
3. The Childhood of Jesus

Chapter Three: Jesus Begins His Ministry

1. Commitment and Gifts
2. Jesus' Baptism
3. The Temptations of Jesus
4. Jesus Begins His Ministry
5. Jesus, The Miracle-Worker

Chapter Four: Jesus and His People

1. Who You Are
2. The Story of Jesus' People
3. Religious Groups in Jesus' Day

Chapter Five: Jesus: The Teacher

1. Living Jesus' Teaching
2. Jesus' Teaching Style
3. Parables
4. Summary of Jesus' Teaching

Chapter Six: Jesus: A Gospel Portrait

1. Jesus, Good News and You
2. Gospel Formation
3. Mark's Jesus: The Servant Messiah
4. Matthew's Jesus: The New Moses
5. Luke's Jesus: Savior of the World
6. John's Jesus: The Word of God

Chapter Seven: Jesus: A Personal Portrait

1. The Human Jesus
2. Jesus as Friend
3. The Strong, Gentle Jesus
4. The Honest, Courageous Jesus
5. Jesus and Women

Chapter Eight: The Paschal Mystery of Jesus:
        Passion, Death and Resurrection

1. A Quiz (The Last Days of Jesus)
2. The Passion Narratives
3. Living Jesus' Passion, Death and Resurrection

Chapter Nine: Belief Through the Ages

1. Faith in Symbol
2. Titles of Jesus
3. Jesus of the Councils
4. The Jesus of the Creed
5. Two Questions About Jesus

Chapter Ten: Meeting the Risen Lord

1. Jesus and You
2. Jesus Lives in You
3. Jesus Lives in the Church
4. Scripture—God's Word
5. Meeting Jesus in Prayer
6. Jesus Lives in Others
7. Conclusion: Who Do *You* Say I Am?

Glossary of Selected Terms

Sequence.   Our own teaching experience of the material of the text suggests that you present the material in the order outlined above. It has worked for us, but you could easily rearrange the sequence along the lines suggested below. In any case, Chapter 1 is introductory and should be treated first.

You could make a case for treating the historical material in Chapter 4 right after Chapter 1. This content, however, may be too "heavy" for the first part of the course. You will be more likely to hold student interest if you "jump right in" with the life of Jesus.

You could also make a case for teaching Chapter 6, which gives an overview of the gospels, before the content of the "life-and-teaching-of-Jesus" chapters (2, 3, 5 and 8). If, like many teachers, you require the thorough reading and study of at least one gospel in a Jesus course, you might prefer to give the introduction to the gospels in the beginning of the course. We might point out that the scripture assignments given in the text require students to read most of the chapters in the synoptic gospels, especially those in Matthew and Luke, and several important chapters and key verses in John.

Finally, you might discuss Chapter 7—the personal portrait of Jesus—at any point in the course where you feel the students have been exposed to enough information to construct their own "portrait" of Jesus.

The entire book should be taught in light of Chapter 10—meeting the risen Lord. It is always good to begin a course with an overview of how and why a text is organized the way it is. You might even have students skim through Chapter 10 early on so they can see where they will end up. This will stress that they are learning about Jesus to grow closer to him and others.

Methods and Media

Each chapter of the Teacher's Manual annotates audiovisual materials you may use to supplement the material of the chapter. We believe in the value of story telling in religious education, especially through good films. Films can be modern parables, so we point you to some outstanding full-length feature films we have successfully used in our own teaching over the years.

Don't forget the cardinal rules for using audiovisuals:

1. *Always preview with an eye toward their suitability for your own students.* In the case of films, although we recognize that students can sometimes benefit from some excellent R-rated films, we think it prudent not to use anything but G- and PG-rated films with high school students. Parents are the prime religious educators, and we should not presume to use materials some parents would find objectionable.

2. *Order materials early to avoid disappointment.*

3. *Follow up your use of an audiovisual with a discussion and some meaningful assignments.* Students should never be given the impression that viewing a film is an excuse to stop thinking. Also, youth are manipulated by the media today with subtle and subliminally persuasive cues. Religious educators can develop in their students a critical eye and judgment concerning the media. This is especially true of Jesus films. Many people have an image of Jesus that comes from films they have seen about him, but not all films are historically or theologically accurate. Critical evaluation of one of the major movies about Jesus could be a major objective of the course.

Here is a list of several methods that we have used in teaching our own Jesus courses:

1. *Discussion, both small and large-group.* Discussion builds Christian community in the classroom and often leads to faith sharing among students.

2. *Lecture and note-taking.* A great lecture on your part can stimulate student interest, introduce difficult material, organize units logically and summarize key ideas. Requiring students to take notes on key points teaches an essential skill that will help them in all their courses. Perhaps you can spend a short session on how to take good notes in your class.

3. *Journal-keeping.* Keeping a journal is a special feature of this course and the entire series. Explain its value to your students, especially as a method of prayer.

4. *Research projects.* Both the student text and this manual suggest several projects your students could do. Many of them deal with critical reading of the gospels.

5. *Guest speakers.* You might invite several guest speakers to witness to what Jesus means to them in their lives.

6. *Interviewing.* Occasionally we suggest that students discuss material with their parents or other adults. This can open up dialogue and help parents exercise their own ministry of religious education.

7. *Values exercises.* Each chapter has at least one key exercise designed to get students to think about Jesus as he relates to their everyday life and values. Be sure to allot time to discuss these.

8. *Faith sharing.* Throughout the course you'll find several opportunities to give personal witness based on your own friendship with Jesus. We are convinced that an enthusiastic, joyful catechist is the key to a successful Jesus course.

9. *Praying.* Each chapter contains a prayer reflection. You'll add to these by using the introductory scriptural quotes and other prayers provided. In addition, student meditations and reflections are suggested for journal entries.

10. *Audiovisuals.* Be sure to use some of these to provide variety and stimulate student interest. We highly recommend that you show one of the major features on Jesus during this course and analyze it critically.

11. *Service project.* Service is an underlying theme of the book. You might devise a class project to be worked on throughout the semester.

12. *Bible reading.* We strongly recommend that students read and study thoroughly at least one gospel in this Christology course, perhaps Matthew or Luke. We have assigned different gospels in different years to help enrich our own teaching of the course.

13. *Article reading.* We strongly recommend that you assign some reading from both popular and more scholarly Catholic magazines. Give your students a list of Catholic periodicals available in your department, school, parish and local libraries. Teach students how to use *The Catholic Periodical and Literature Index.* A suggested assignment is to have them read three or four articles on

a given topic, for example, Jesus' self-understanding, and report their research in a short paper.

14. *Text reading and summarizing.*

Evaluation

We believe in evaluation and grading in Catholic high school religious education. Evaluation determines whether objectives are being met. If good teaching happens, then learning is taking place, too.

The quizzes and tests included in this manual as well as ones that you will devise yourself offer a good means of evaluation. Other ways to judge the effectiveness of your teaching and student learning include observing student attention in class; participation; the quality of student questions and responses; journal entries; fidelity to homework assignments; participation in service projects; cooperation with you and fellow students; participation in prayer; personal interviews with each student and informal interaction.

In religious education courses we teach to the cognitive ("head" knowledge), affective ("heart" knowledge), and the behavioral ("feet" or action knowledge) domains. Student performance in all these areas should be reflected in the grade you assign for the course.

Assigning grades in religion courses symbolically states to students the importance of religion classes. Grades should never be used to manipulate, control or intimidate students. In Christian charity and justice, many opportunities should be given for students to do well. Grasp of cognitive content should not be the exclusive criterion for grades. We believe in rewarding students for effort, participation and cooperation.

Structure of the Teacher's Manual

Each chapter of this manual includes:

Introduction: A brief overview of the content, approach and rationale of the chapter.

Further Reading for the Teacher: A short annotated bibliography of works that could serve as useful background for you. We sometimes suggest good books for your students as well.

Suggested Audiovisual Ideas: We list some references in each chapter. One could make a full-time study of keeping up with materials produced each year and that are available for classroom use. Videocassette formatting has eased our job in many ways. Be sure your department is on the mailing list of AV producers and read the reviews of new materials in publications like *The Catechist* and *Religion Teacher's Journal.* Many motion picture distributors will gladly send you their catalogue. We have found *Using Media in Religious Education* by Ronald Sarno (Birmingham, AL: Religious Education Press, 1987) very helpful.

Objectives: Behavioral objectives are targeted to observable tasks students can perform, such as recalling, explaining and summarizing information. Expressive objectives appeal to the affective domain and include goals like appreciation, valuing, reflection and praying.

The objectives helped to dictate what was included in the particular chapter. You will, of course, supplement these with your own objectives to meet the needs of your students.

Time Used and Procedure: A suggested procedure for teaching each chapter is included. Veteran teachers might use very little of this procedure as they draw on their own repertoire of teaching techniques and years of experience. Novice teachers might depend more on the techniques suggested here.

The Teacher's Manual includes supplementary exercises and assignments not included in the student text. Some of these are reprinted at the end of this manual in a Tear-Out Section so that you can easily duplicate them for your students.

We envision this text as the basis of a semester course, perhaps meeting each day for a 45-minute class. The text includes a number of exercises and writing assignments that could serve as homework assignments.

We suggest a time-frame for the teaching of each chapter but this can vary widely depending on several variables: the quality of discussion; the number of films and other audiovisuals you use; the celebrating of liturgical activities like a class Mass; days set aside for library or in-class research projects; or the use of guest speakers.

The key word is *adaptability.* You don't have to use everything. Please pick, choose, supplement—adapt. Your own experience is the best guide.

Parish Religious Education Adaptation: We try to suggest ways you can convert the key content of each chapter into a 90-minute class.

The text and the Teacher's Manual include enough exercises and activities that you can easily adapt it for more classes or for longer sessions. For example, some programs meeting on a monthly or bi-weekly basis could easily incorporate a feature film for discussion and application to the themes of a particular chapter.

If you use the text with students in parish religious education programs, please study the various ideas in the **Procedure** sections of this manual. This section will contain some ideas you can use with your students.

chapter 1
Jesus
Who Is This Person?

■ introduction ■

The study of Jesus is central to our Catholic faith. Christian discipleship forms the basis of our church. Chapter 1 introduces the student to the historical person of Jesus and his significance in human history. The opening exercise can provide the teacher with an idea of where the students are on their faith journey.

It is necessary to clarify student belief in Jesus as a historical person. The section "Did Jesus Exist?" demonstrates that there was indeed a historical Jesus on whom Christian faith is reliably based. The chapter offers some evidence from both Roman and Jewish sources to validate the gospels as accurate witnesses to the life of Jesus.

We think it is important for students to realize that faith in Jesus is not irrational; it is crucial that there was a real, historical Jesus. Contrary to what some believe, the Christian message is rooted in a real person who suffered and died for us.

The chapter also introduces both friendly and hostile contemporaries of Jesus. These help to provide a historical context for Jesus' life. The chapter concludes with four "Catholic" answers to Jesus' question: "Who do people say that I am?"

Perhaps you could have several pictures of Jesus, a crucifix and a set of bibles available in the classroom. We recommend either the New American Bible or the Jerusalem Bible.

Further Reading for the Teacher

Bligh, John. *Historical Information for New Testament Students*. Baltimore: Helicon, 1965.

Excellent outline treatment of the historical facts necessary to understand the biblical story of Jesus.

Brown, S. S., Raymond, Fitzmyer, S. J., Joseph and Murphy, O. Carm., Roland, eds. *The Jerome Biblical Commentary*. Englewood Cliffs, NJ: Prentice-Hall, 1969.

An outstanding one-volume commentary which includes interesting entries on many topics useful to the study of Christology, for example, "Aspects of New Testament Thought."

Bruce, F. F. *Jesus and Christian Origins Outside the New Testament*. Grand Rapids, MI: William B. Eerdmans, 1974.

This book is rich background with its treatment of New Testament origins and belief in Jesus as it relates to extra-biblical evidence. Highly recommended.

Cornfeld, Gaalyah. *The Historical Jesus: A Scholarly View of the Man and His World*. New York: MacMillan, 1982.

Helpful background reading.

Habermas, Gary R. *The Verdict of History: Conclusive Evidence for the Life of Jesus*. Nashville, TN: Thomas Nelson, 1988.

Offers good data to help teach the historical Christ.

McCauley, Michael F. *The Jesus Book*. Chicago: Thomas More Press, 1978.

A variety of artistic representations and descriptions of Jesus through the ages.

McKenzie, John L. *Dictionary of the Bible*. New York: Macmillan, 1967.

A classic which is still quite useful.

O'Collins, Gerald. *Interpreting Jesus*. Mahwah, NJ: Paulist Press, 1983.

We'd recommend this book over any other as background for teaching the student text. It is scholarly, balanced and orthodox.

Pfeifer, Carl J. *Teaching Jesus Today*. Mystic, CT: Twenty-Third Publications, 1981.

Some good essays on the various presences of Jesus. The teaching recommendations are quite good.

Rouet, Albert. *A Short Dictionary of the New Testament*. Mahwah, NJ: Paulist Press, 1982.

A useful resource.

Wijngaards, John. *Handbook to the Gospels*. Ann Arbor, MI: Servant Publications, 1983.

A delightful, easy-to-read introduction to the gospels with much interesting background information on Jesus and his times.

Suggested Audiovisual Ideas

The Bible: What's It All About? Part 5, "What Is the New Testament?" (30-minute, videocassette, Teleketics). Good for the early grades of high school; an introduction to the New Testament as the good news of the risen Jesus.

The Faces of Jesus (10-minute color film, Carousel Films). A visual collage of Jesus in art through the ages.

The Man (30-minute, videocassette/16mm film, Mass Media Ministries). This short presentation specifically addresses the question: Who did Jesus say he was?

T.V. The Anonymous Teacher (16-minute color film, Mass Media Ministries). Shows how television sells values.

The Three Questions (14-minute, 16mm animation, Mass Media Ministries). Based on a Tolstoy folktale; provides a good introduction to the course by pondering three fundamental questions.

Objectives

That students . . .

1. *Appreciate* the significance of Jesus Christ in human history.
2. *Examine* their own beliefs about Jesus.
3. *Identify, analyze* and *interpret* several non-biblical references to Jesus.
4. *Confirm* the historicity of Jesus and the reliability of the gospels.
5. *Distinguish* between "knowing about" Jesus and "knowing" Jesus.
6. *Familiarize* themselves with the contemporaries of Jesus such as Herod the Great, Pilate and John the Baptist.
7. *Respond* to the question, "Who do you say that I am?"

Time Used

Allow at least seven classes to cover the material of this chapter.

Procedure

Session 1: **Introduction**

1. Begin class with the scripture reading that opens the chapter. Pray spontaneously to the Lord, asking him to guide you on your journey to better knowledge of him.
2. Discuss the impact of Jesus on history. Use the following questions:
    — How would history have changed?
    — Would the students be in class right now if Jesus hadn't lived?
    — Would there be any "Lives of the Saints"?
    — Would America have become the United States?

— Has any historical figure had more impact than Jesus?

— What does this say about the value of earthly power, wealth and prestige?

3. Distinguish between "knowing about" and "knowing" Jesus using Father DeMello's story at the beginning of the chapter.

4. Have students work the exercise "Who Do You Say I Am?" Discuss and begin the journal exercise.

5. *Optional Assignment*: Have the students look at home or in the library for a story, saying or prayer that speaks of Jesus. Perhaps you can post these on the bulletin board. Allow a few days for the completion of this assignment.

Session 2: **Jesus in Music**

1. Begin this lesson by explaining that Jesus has captured the imaginations of people throughout history. Music is one medium they have chosen to express their relationship to the Lord. Brainstorm to come up with any songs the students might know about Jesus.

2. Present a series of musical selections that cover different styles of music and different perspectives on God and Jesus. Use the following worksheet. (These are just some possible choices; use any that are available.)

Selection	Place	Time	Style	Perspective
Antiphons (Choir of the Carmelite Priory)	church or monastery	Middle Ages	Gregorian chant	Revere God; music is sacred and simple
Jesu, Joy of Man's Desiring	church	18–19th centuries	classical hymn	majestic and reverential treatment of Jesus
Take Our Bread	church	1960s	folk guitar	personal relationship to a loving God
Everything's Alright	stage and film	1970s	modern threatrical	a human Jesus emphasized
El Shaddai (Amy Grant)	concert/ album	1980s	Christian rock	a God of history: Jesus the savior
Shower the People	concert	1970s	secular/ religious	emphasis on message of Christ rather than the person

3. Discuss some of these songs (or others) while filling in the information on the chart (as the sample above) on the board or overhead. Encourage students to

bring various songs to class for your introductory prayer during the coming days as you cover the material of this chapter.

Session 3: The Historical Jesus (A Pre-Test)

1. Begin by reading the following selection and doing the exercises below.

For your convenience in duplicating, the following material is reprinted on page 138 of the tear-out section in the teacher's manual.

One Solitary Life

Here is a young man who was born in an obscure village, the child of a peasant woman.

He worked in a carpenter shop until he was thirty.

He never wrote a book. He never held an office. He never owned a home. He never had a family. He never went to college.

He never did one of the things that usually accompany greatness. He had no credentials but himself.

While he was still a young man the tide of public opinion turned against him. His friends ran away. He was turned over to his enemies.... He was nailed to a cross between two thieves.

While he was dying, his executioners gambled for the only piece of property he had on earth, and that was his coat. When he was dead, he was laid in a borrowed grave through the pity of a friend.

Nineteen centuries have come and gone, and today he is . . . the leader of the column of progress. I am far within the mark when I say that all the armies that ever marched, and all the kings that ever reigned, have not affected the life of man upon this earth as has this One Solitary Life.

Relationship with Jesus. How are you doing in your relationship with Jesus? Judge your life with Jesus by writing your initials on the point on the dotted line which best represents where you are with him right now.

1. active . . . . .passive

2. exciting . . . . .dull

3. close . . . . .distant

4. friendly . . . . .stranger

5. deeply . . . . .shallow
   personal   & cold

Discuss:

1. If Jesus were to appear to you, what one question would you like to ask him?

2. Share several of the questions you and your classmates would like to ask Jesus. Imagine how he might answer them. Decide where you might go to find additional information.

3. Because some of your students are convinced that history is dry and uninteresting, part of our catechetical task is to help them see that our faith in Christ depends on an exciting historical person. We need to create a desire in students to learn more about him.

   Challenge the class to answer the following pre-test questions. This usually arouses student interest and counteracts their charge that "we've heard this all before."

   You could give this in oral or written form.

For your convenience in duplicating, the following material is reprinted on page 139 of the tear-out section in the teacher's manual.

Jesus Pre-test

Fill in the blanks:

1. What does the name *Jesus* mean? _____

2. What was Jesus' profession? _____

3. Name several of his relatives: _____

4. Where was he born? When? _____

5. What might he have looked like? _____

6. How much formal religious education did he have? _____

   _____

7. What was his nationality? his religion? _____

8. Where did he live? _____

9. How old was he when he died? _____

10. Who were his best friends? _____

True or False

_____ 11. Jesus experienced temptation to do evil as we do.

_____ 12. From the time he was a child, Jesus knew everything there was to know because he was also God.

_____ 13. Jesus was like us in *all* things except sin.

_____ 14. While he was on earth, Jesus started the church with a pope and bishops, just like we have today.

_____ 15. The gospels were written when the apostles were with Jesus.

_____ 16. Jesus' main proclamation was "the kingdom of God."

_____ 17. Jesus got angry at certain things and people.

_____ 18. Sometimes Jesus didn't follow all the rules of the Jewish religion.

_____ 19. Because he was God, Jesus really didn't have to eat and sleep each day.

_____ 20. Jesus knew the exact future before it occurred because he was God.

Answers

1. Yahweh is salvation
2. carpenter/teacher/healer
3. Mary, Joseph, John the Baptist
4. Bethlehem (6–4 B.C.)
5. an Aramaic Jew of Palestine, with dark skin and a beard, rugged carpenter
6. training as a rabbi
7. Aramaic Jew
8. Nazareth in Galilee
9. between 33–36 years of age
10. the apostles, disciples, and outcasts

11. true
12. false
13. true
14. false
15. false
16. true
17. true
18. true
19. false
20. false

3. Review the pre-test and discuss any points of interest. Some of the answers to the first ten questions are reviewed in this chapter. Rate them on the following scale:

20/19 correct: "You will be a saint some day!"

18/17 correct: "You would make a great pope."

16/15 correct: "You'd make a great apostle."

14/13 correct: "You'd make a great disciple."

12/0 correct: "This course is for you!"

Session 4: **Did Jesus Exist?**

1. The first section of the chapter covers five non-biblical sources that help verify the historicity of Jesus. As you cover this material, make a chart on the board that covers the following information. You might have students copy this into their notebooks.

Name	Date	Document	What This Tells Us About Jesus
Suetonius			
Tacitus			
Pliny			
Josephus			
Babylonian Talmud			

2. When treating the Josephus quote, have students figure out for themselves why a non-Christian Jew would not be likely to have written the passage attributed to Josephus.

3. After working through this material, discuss the questions that appear on page 14.

4. Discuss how the non-biblical material verifies the gospels. This helps show that the gospels were not "made-up fantasy," but based on historical fact.

5. You might have students read the next section of the chapter for homework.

Session 5: **Friend or Foe?**

1. Explain that Jesus' message is so powerful that it radically challenges us either to accept or reject it. Therefore, both in biblical times and now, people are either for or against Jesus.

2. Recall the various portraits of Jesus in the section, "Jesus and His Contemporaries." Have students discuss and then categorize these people as either *for* or *against* Jesus. Do this exercise after students have done the various gospel readings suggested throughout this section of the chapter.

For your convenience in duplicating, the following material is reprinted on page 140 of the tear-out section in the teacher's manual.

Friend or Foe?

Name	Identify	For/ against
1. Herod Antipas		
2. John the Baptist		
3. Caiaphas		
4. Scribes		
5. Gamaliel		

Name	Identify	For/ against
6. Pharisees		
7. the Magi		
8. Herod the Great		
9. Pontius Pilate		

For further discussion, list some other people who have expressed opinions about Jesus and religion. Examples include:

Friedrich Nietzsche: argued that "God is dead"

Jean Vanier: sees Jesus in the mentally and physically disabled

Karl Marx: saw religion as the opiate of the people

Hugh Hefner: glorifies sexual indulgence

Mohandas Gandhi: greatly admired Jesus but could not understand luke-warm Christians

3. *Assignment*:   Ask students to research one quote from a book of quotations from a famous person to see what that person said about Jesus.

Session 6: **Modern Views of Jesus**

1. Allow time for students to share and discuss the results of their research.

2. Discuss the contemporary theological views of Jesus treated in the last section of this chapter.

3. Read through the quotes from Matthew 25 and the examples given in the text. For each one of these, come up with three more examples. List them on the board. (See discussion question on page 22).

4. *Assignment*:   Be sure to have students do the interview assignment in the journal entry at the end of this section.

Session 7: **Quiz on Chapter One**

1. Begin class with the Prayer Reflection at the end of the chapter.

2. Review the material of the chapter. Perhaps students could work on the focus questions in small groups. You might use the following quiz as a short check on student mastery of the material:

For your convenience in duplicating, the following material is reprinted on page 141 of the tear-out section in the teacher's manual.

Quiz on Chapter 1

Name: _____

Date: _____

Multiple Choice: Choose the letter that best completes the statement.

_____ 1. The primary source of information about the existence of Jesus: (A) the Evangelists; (B) Pliny the Younger; (C) Suetonius; (D) Josephus.

_____ 2. This Jewish historian referred to Jesus in his historical writings: (A) Tacitus; (B) Suetonius; (C) Josephus; (D) Pliny the Younger.

_____ 3. The town where Jesus grew up: (A) Bethlehem; (B) Nazareth; (C) Jerusalem; (D) Samaria.

_____ 4. The image of Jesus that portrays him as a liberator: (A) Person for Others; (B) Way to Freedom; (C) Savior; (D) Human Face of God.

_____ 5. The person who gave a faith-filled response to Jesus' question "Who do you say that I am?" (A) Gamaliel; (B) Peter; (C) Caiaphas (D) Mark.

_____ 6. The fifth Roman prefect in Judea: (A) John the Baptist; (B) Pontius Pilate; (C) Caiaphas; (D) Hillel.

_____ 7. This person might have been related to the Essenes' desert community; he was a precursor of the Messiah. (A) John the Baptist; (B) Pontius Pilate; (C) Caiaphas; (D) Peter.

_____ 8. The high priest of the Jerusalem Temple: (A) Josephus; (B) Thaddeus; (C) Caiaphas; (D) Joseph of Arimathea.

_____ 9. The "separated ones," who observed the Law strictly: (A) Sadducees; (B) Essenes; (C) Sanhedrin; (D) Pharisees.

_____ 10. The image of Jesus that stresses his example of true human living: (A) Way to Freedom; (B) Savior; (C) Human Face of God; (D) Person for Others.

Short Essay: At this stage of your life, who do you say that Jesus is?

Answers:

1.	A	6.	B
2.	C	7.	A
3.	B	8.	C
4.	B	9.	D
5.	B	10.	C

Adaptation for Parish Religious Education Classes

Step 1: **Introduction** (15 minutes)

1. Begin with the opening scripture reading. Then read Father DeMello's story about the "saved man."

2. Introduce the course, and then ask students to work on the exercise "Who Do You Say I Am?"

Step 2: **The Historical Jesus** (20 minutes)

1. Ask students why it is important to believe in a historical Jesus.

2. Then, briefly comment on some of the "proofs" for Jesus' historical existence outside of the New Testament.

Step 3: **What Jesus' Contemporaries Thought of Him** (30 minutes)

1. Provide each student with a copy of the New Testament.

2. Before class, select some passages from the gospels that reveal what certain contemporaries of Jesus thought of him. Give each student one or more of these passages to check out.

3. Have them read the passage and note what it says. They could then read additional material from the text if applicable. They should prepare and then give a short report on what they found.

Step 4: **Contemporary View(s) of Jesus** (25 minutes)

1. As time permits, briefly touch on the four images of Jesus discussed in the chapter.

2. We highly recommend that you take up the image "Jesus: Way to Freedom" and read and discuss together the Matthew 25 allusions. Discuss the question on page 22.

You might ask the students to interview one peer and two adults on who they think Jesus is and be prepared to report to the class at the next session.

chapter 2
Jesus
The Early Years

▪ *introduction* ▪

It is often wise to begin at the beginning. Although the infancy narratives of Jesus were written about 70 years after the events occurred, they provide an introduction to both the gospels and the story of Jesus. By asking the questions what, when, where, who, how and why, this chapter provides valuable historical and geographical information on Jesus.

The chapter begins by setting the birth of Jesus in the context of a gift that God has given us. The students are challenged to examine other gifts God has given them using the exercise, "You Are Gift!"

The birth narratives are presented as stories that make *theological* statements about Jesus rather than being strictly historical accounts. This section of the chapter addresses key questions such as:

What is taking place in the birth of Jesus?

When was Jesus born?

Where was Jesus born?

Who? What does the name Jesus mean?

How was Jesus conceived?

The chapter concludes with Matthew's and Luke's stories about Jesus' childhood. He lived the typical life of Jewish children of his day, despite the wisdom he demonstrated in the Temple. We end the chapter by asking the students to examine their obedience to their parents.

Further Reading for the Teacher

Brown, S. S., Raymond E. *The Birth of the Messiah.* New York: Doubleday Image, 1979.

> A scholarly examination of the infancy narratives of Matthew and Luke.

Brown, S. S., Raymond E. *The Virginal Conception and Bodily Resurrection of Jesus.* Mahwah, NJ: Paulist Press, 1973.

> Brown is an excellent Catholic scholar—here he tackles two controversial issues debated in academic circles. Excellent insights into the virgin birth.

Chesterton, G. K. *The Everlasting Man.* New York: Doubleday, 1974.

> Chesterton traces history from a Catholic perspective; his insights into the birth of Jesus are invaluable. Read especially the chapter entitled, "God in the Cave."

O'Rourke, O. P., David K. *The Holy Land as Jesus Knew It: Its People, Customs and Religion.* Liguori, MO: Liguori Publications, 1983.

> Excellent and well-illustrated background reading.

Reader's Digest Editors. *Mysteries of the Bible: The Enduring Questions of the Scriptures.* Pleasantville, NY: The Reader's Digest Association, Inc., 1988.

> Excellent, thumbnail sketches on biblical themes, including many vignettes from the life of Jesus. Students will enjoy this one.

Suggested Audiovisual Ideas

Bible Map Transparencies (10 transparencies, Broadman Films). Good geographical overlays.

Biblical Locations in Galilee Today (35-minute color filmstrip with cassette and printed key, ACTA Foundation). Produced by Francis Filas, S.J. Overview of the places Jesus visited during his earthly ministry. Shows many of the contemporary shrines. You might also look at Father Filas' *Jerusalem: 66 A.D.* (42-minute filmstrip, also from ACTA) which shows a scale model of Jerusalem before the revolt.

The Birth of Jesus (30-minute, videocassette, Teleketics). A guided tour of places in the Holy Land involved in the birth story of Jesus.

"Born For Us," *Jesus of Nazareth* (28-minute, 16mm, Part 2 of 14, Don Bosco Multimedia). The infancy narratives in Matthew and Luke are shown in this excerpt from the classic film.

Christ In His Own Land, Part 4 (26-minute, color film, Don Bosco Multimedia). Covers Bethlehem and the Flight to Egypt using excerpts from the gospel narratives.

The Fourth Wise Man (48-minute, videocassette, Paulist Productions). A fictional presentation on a "fourth" wise man in search of the Messiah.

The Giving Tree (10-minute, 16mm animated, ROA). A parable that demonstrates the unconditional love of God. Can be used to supplement the introductory story.

I Have A Dream: The Life of Dr. Martin Luther King, Jr. (35-minute, 16mm, Mass Media Ministries). A stirring documentary on the life of King. A good parallel of a "king" in the contemporary world.

Jesus, B.C. (27.5-minute color film, Paulist Productions). A parable on the Incarnation. Reviews the salvation history of the Old Testament in an allegorical way.

Where Jesus Walked (26-minute color film, Brigham Young University). A fine film focusing on Jesus' life.

Objectives

That students . . .

1. *Understand* the theological importance of the birth stories of Jesus.
2. *Appreciate* the gift God gave us in Jesus.
3. *Distinguish* between the two genealogies given in the gospels of Matthew and Luke.
4. *Compare* and *contrast* Luke's and Matthew's infancy narratives.
5. *Know* the meaning of the name Jesus.
6. *Familiarize* themselves with the symbols in Matthew's and Luke's infancy narratives.
7. *Identify* the key geographical sites of Palestine.
8. *Review* Old Testament prophecies that relate to the birth of Jesus.

Time Used

Allow at least eight days for this chapter. The map exercise will take at least two days. The scavenger hunt may need an extra day to complete and review the data.

Procedure

Session 1: **Introduction**

1. Begin class by playing a traditional Christmas carol or hymn.
2. Together with the students, read the paraphrased version of "The Gift of the Magi" that introduces the chapter. Mention the greatness of God's gift to us in Jesus. (You might ask them to do their own version of this story.)
3. Work the exercise "You Are Gift!" Allow time for sharing.
4. *Optional assignment*:   You may want to assign this little exercise to underscore the importance of the birth of Jesus and its place in history. Have the students research the origins of the following carols or examine the theology the hymns contain.

1. Silent Night	6. O Little Town of Bethlehem
2. O Holy Night	7. O Come All Ye Faithful
3. What Child Is This?	8. God Rest Ye Merry Gentlemen
4. O Come, O Come Immanuel	9. Glory to God (Handel's *Messiah*)
5. Away in a Manger	10. Hallelujah Chorus (Handel's *Messiah*)

A helpful resource: Carol Ward, *The Christian Sourcebook* (New York: Ballantine Books, 1986), pp. 7-8. This resource also has some good background material on various Christmas customs.

Have the students share their findings with the rest of the class.

Session 2: **Family Ties: What Does Jesus' Birth Mean?**

1. Examine the two genealogies in Matthew and Luke. Ask the students to suggest any similarities or differences. List them on the board.

2. Explain to the students that the infancy narratives try to say something about Jesus and who he was. They are theological rather than strictly historical. Draw out some theological conclusions, for example:

Luke: tried to show that Jesus is the universal Messiah.

Matthew: traced Jesus to Abraham and David to show that Jesus' coming fulfilled God's promises to the Jewish people.

3. You might want to use the following handout for supplementary work:

For your convenience in duplicating, the following material is reprinted on page 142 of the tear-out section in the teacher's manual.

Family Ties

Examine Matthew's genealogy carefully. You'll find there something almost unheard of in Jewish genealogies of Jesus' day—the names of *women*. These aren't just any women either, but well-known Old Testament characters whose reputations would make the reader think twice. What are they doing in Jesus' family tree? For example, there is Tamar, a Canaanite woman who donned the dress of a prostitute to seduce her father-in-law Judah and bear his son (Genesis 38). Or take Rahab, another prostitute. She hid Joshua's spies in Jericho, thus helping the Israelites conquer the Promised Land (Joshua 2). Ruth is a final example. She was a non-Jew, a Moabite, who followed the advice of Naomi and charmed the wealthy Boaz into marrying her.

To Jesus' contemporaries, these women were symbols of determination, quick-wittedness and faith. Yahweh showered his blessings on Gentiles, adopted them into the family of his Chosen People and used them to fulfill his promises.

Assignment:

All of us should study our family trees to learn about the fascinating people who are part of our own story. Construct your own family tree as far back as you can. Be sure to interview grandparents and great-grandparents to find out some of the interesting details in the story of your family. Please share with your classmates at least three new things you discovered about your family heritage.

Journal:

Write a two-page biography of a significant woman in your life—your mother or one of your grandmothers. Discuss three of her best qualities. Report how you are like her or different from her. Write about what she means to you.

4. *Optional Approach*: To plan for covering the material in the chapter, you might want to divide your students into six equal groups. Have them read the six sections and report back to the group. They should address one of the following:

     #1 *What* is taking place in the birth of Jesus?

     #2 *When* was Jesus born?

     #3 *Where* was Jesus born?

     #4 *Who?* What does the name Jesus mean?

     #5 *How* was Jesus born?

     #6 *Why* was Jesus born?

Session 3: **What's in a Name?**

1. For opening prayer, use "El Shaddai" by Amy Grant. Make note of the line "by the power of your name."

2. Remind students of the Hebrew notion that to know a person's name gave you power. (This may explain why salespeople often want to know your name.) In Exodus, God refuses to give a personal name. He reveals the highly enigmatic word *Yahweh*, meaning "I am who I am." Some scholars understand this to be a refusal to give a name; thus, Yahweh remains all-powerful and transcendent. In Jesus' time, the name of God was so important that it was not allowed to be spoken in ordinary conversation.

3. Ask the students to give examples of names they use to try to have power over each other. (You may need to warn them about vulgarity.)

4. Review the historical data on pages 34–35 about the name *Jesus*.

5. Work the following exercise. Students might do this in groups. Be sure to have books on the meaning of names on hand. These are readily available at local libraries. We sometimes search out the meaning of the surnames of our students. We can't find all of them, but we find enough to impress and interest them in this topic. The "Challenge" exercise will get them talking to their grandparents.

For your convenience in duplicating, the following material is reprinted on page 143 of the tear-out section in the teacher's manual.

What's in a Name?

A person's name helps root that person in history. It says "Here is a real person with this set of parents, with this occupation, from this place." Every

Christian name carries some significance. For example, here are some common biblical names with their meanings:

David — beloved of God

Ann — full of grace

Michael — he who is like God

John — God is gracious

Ruth — a beautiful friend

Joseph — let God add

Using a book on names as a reference, research the meaning of your first and middle name:

Name: _____ **Meaning:** _____

Name: _____ **Meaning:** _____

If you bear the name of a Christian saint, prepare a brief report on his or her life. If you are not named after a Christian saint, report on the life of your favorite saint. *The New Catholic Encyclopedia*, *Butler's Lives of the Saints* or some other book on the saints should be of help. Share your research in a report to the class.

Challenge:

Find the meaning of your surname. Perhaps your parents or grandparents would know what it means. Your public library should have books on last names you can use for reference. Does your surname tell you about an ancestral profession, place of residence, a physical attribute or first name of an ancestor? Does this help to give you a sense of identity and pride in your family?

Session 4: **Old Testament Prophecies**

1. Recall any Old Testament prophecies used in standard Christmas songs. (Refer to the list in Session 1.)

2. Explain that Matthew and Luke used many Old Testament images in order to show that, from the beginning of Jesus' life, he was the new Messiah.

3. Have the students research the following ten passages from the Old Testament. Have them identify how the passage relates to Jesus:

Passages	*Answers*
#1 Isaiah 7:14	the virgin birth of Immanuel
#2 Isaiah 9:5	images of Jesus— Wonder-Counselor Mighty-God Eternal-Father Prince-of-Peace
#3 Jeremiah 31:31	New Covenant
#4 Ezekiel 34:11–12	Good Shepherd
#5 Micah 5:1–3	Bethlehem
#6 Zechariah 9:9	riding on a donkey
#7 Numbers 24:17	star

Passages	*Answers*
#8 Exodus 1:15–22	slaughter of the innocents
#9 Wisdom 7:4–6	swaddling clothing
#10 Psalm 72:10	the three kings

Session 5: **Map Exercise: Where Was Jesus born?**

1. This is an excellent time to show one of the short films on the Holy Land. Here are a couple assignments you might find helpful:

    a. *Slides*: As a small-group activity, encourage students to make their own slides of the Holy Land. Using a Visual Maker (like one from Kodak), students can make high-quality slides by taking photos from biblical atlases, back issues of *National Geographic* and the like. Twenty slides can be made inexpensively. Magazines can also be a source for homemade slides using clear contact paper and slide mounts. Students have responded well to this assignment.

    b. Using good biblical atlases, you can assign the following map exercise:

For your convenience in duplicating, the following material is reprinted on page 144 of the tear-out section in the teacher's manual.

Map Exercise

Locate the following places on a map of the Holy Land. Then, read the references given below. In the space provided, mention how the particular locale figured in Jesus' ministry.

Cana (John 2:1–12) _____

_____

Capernaum (Matthew 4:12–17) _____

_____

Jordan River (John 1:19–34) _____

_____

Emmaus (Luke 24:13–35) _____

_____

Bethany (Matthew 26:6–13) _____

Using a good bible atlas (for example, *The Macmillan Bible Atlas*), find a map of Jerusalem in Jesus' day. Use it to outline the Temple and indicate the various places of interest during the last week of Jesus' life.

Session 6: **Birth Narratives**

1. Begin by listening to "New Star Shining" by Ricky Skaggs and James Taylor.
2. Explain that the birth narratives are more *theological* than *historical*. The focus is Jesus as the risen Christ.
3. Have students research the birth narratives and complete the following checklist:

Identify Where the Following Are Located

_____ 1. star

_____ 2. virgin birth

_____ 3. slaughter of the innocents

_____ 4. flight to Egypt

_____ 5. stable

_____ 6. word made flesh

_____ 7. Bethlehem

_____ 8. angels

_____ 9. shepherds

_____ 10. magi/kings/wise men

MARK

MATTHEW

LUKE

JOHN

BOTH (Matthew and Luke)

4. *Assignment*: Have the students design a crossword puzzle using the following clues. This will serve to review the stories. Have them work each other's puzzle for further review.

For your convenience in duplicating, the following material is reprinted on page 145 of the tear-out section in the teacher's manual.

Crossword Puzzle Clues

1. Temple
2. Herod the Great

3. Egypt

4. gold
5. incense

6. myrrh

7. Bethlehem
8. star
9. stable

A. the great building project of Herod the Great
B. cruel king who slaughtered the Innocents in Bethlehem
C. place of sanctuary for Joseph, Mary and the baby Jesus
D. a gift of the magi: worthy of a king
E. a gift of the magi: burnt offering to God
F. a gift of the magi: an ointment used to prepare a body for burial
G. Joseph's ancestral hometown
H. the sign to the magi of Jesus' birth
I. location of Jesus' birth

10. shepherds	J. the common witnesses to Jesus' birth
11. Jesus	K. name that means "Yahweh is salvation"
12. Nazareth	L. Jesus' hometown in the province of Galilee
13. Incarnation	M. "God becoming human in Jesus"
14. Annunciation	N. the angel Gabriel appearing to Mary
15. Virgin Birth	O. Mary conceiving and bearing Jesus by the power of the Holy Spirit

Session 7: **Jesus' Childhood**

1. Listen to "Voice of the Child" by Michael Card as a reflection on Jesus in the Temple.

2. Using the text, have the students find the three religious rituals involved in the birth of a Jewish male. Review:

   Circumcision: eighth day after birth; given the name Jesus; ritual of entry into the Jewish faith

   Purification: 40 days after birth; Mary becomes ritually clean

   Presentation: first-born is consecrated to God

3. Discuss Jesus' childhood and parallel his to the students. What are the similarities and differences?

4. Work the exercise entitled "Obedience" on page 41 and use the "discuss" questions to begin discussion.

Session 8: **Literary Scavenger Hunt**

1. To review the data of this chapter, have the students work the following scavenger.

For your convenience in duplicating, the following material is reprinted on pages 146–147 of the tear-out section in the teacher's manual.

How Many of These Can You Do in 30 Minutes?

1. The name Jesus means _____.

2. Two points learned from the virginal conception: _____

   _____

3. Jesus' hometown is _____.

4. Jesus was probably born in _____ ⟨place⟩.

5. Luke traces Jesus' genealogy to _____.

6. Nazareth is located in the province of _____.

7. _____ is a Jewish rite where a 13-year old becomes a "son of the Law."

8. Jesus probably studied the _____ like other 5-year-old boys.

9. The _____ was a place of Jewish assembly an worship.

10. Two words of Aramaic that Jesus spoke: _____.

11. In Matthew, God's protection of his Son is symbolized by the flight to _____.

12. Both _____ and _____ recognized Jesus as the Messiah during Jesus' presentation in the Temple.

13. The term meaning God becoming man in Jesus is _____.

14. The angel _____ visits Mary in Luke's gospel.

15. The word *bar* means _____ in the phrase "Jesus bar Mary."

16. The English equivalent of the Greek word meaning "Messiah" or "Anointed One" is _____.

17. The title _____, from Isaiah, means "God is with us."

18. *Jesus* is a late form of the Hebrew name _____.

19. The Jews believed that the Messiah would come from _____'s descendants.

20. Bethlehem is in the province of _____.

21. The gifts of _____, _____, and _____, are symbols used in Matthew's infancy narrative.

22. The ruthless king of Judea, _____, was a volatile mixture of policy and passion.

23. Psalm _____ refers to three kings honoring the Messiah.

24. The Emperor at the time of Jesus' birth was _____.

25. Matthew was primarily writing to a _____-Christian audience.

26. Luke was primarily writing to a _____-Christian audience.

27. The gospel infancy narratives are more _____ than historical.

28. Jesus' genealogy reveals two important truths: Jesus is both _____ and _____.

Answers:

1. Yahweh is salvation
2. (1) Jesus is the unique Son of God; (2) Jesus is a human being like us
3. Nazareth
4. Bethlehem
5. Adam
6. Galilee
7. Bar Mitzvah
8. Torah

9. Synagogue

10. Abba - Talitha koum

11. Egypt

12. Simeon and Anna

13. Incarnation

14. Gabriel

15. son of

16. Christ

17. Immanuel

18. Joshua

19. David

20. Judea

21. gold, frankincense, myrrh

22. Herod the Great

23. 72

24. Caesar Augustus

25. Jewish

26. Gentile

27. theological

28. God and human

2. Review the answers after the 30-minute period and assign extra credit or some bonus to the winning team/person.

Adaptation for Parish Religious Education Classes

Step 1: **Introduction** (30 minutes)

1. Begin with a traditional Christmas song or choose:

    "New Star Shining" — Ricky Skaggs/James Taylor

    "Emmanuel" — Amy Grant

    "Home By Another Way" — James Taylor

2. Read the paraphrased O. Henry story, "The Gift of the Magi," that begins the chapter. Emphasize how great is God's gift to us in Jesus.

3. Work together the "You Are Gift!" exercise. Allow time for sharing.

Step 2: **The Infancy Narratives** (60 minutes)

1. Introduce the narratives by emphasizing that they are primarily *theological* and not strictly historical.

2. Divide the students into 6 groups. Have each group review and report on the following questions:

    a. *What* is taking place in the birth of Jesus?

    b. *When* was Jesus born?

    c. *Where* was Jesus born?

    d. *Who?* What does the name Jesus mean?

    e. *How* was Jesus born?

    f. *Why* was Jesus born?

3. Review the data they present in the reports and answer any questions they may have.

4. Work either the *Checklist*, the *Crossword Project*, or the *Scavenger Hunt* to familiarize the students with the content of Matthew's and Luke's infancy narratives.

5. *Optional*: Show a short film on the Holy Land.

chapter 3

Jesus Begins His Ministry

▪ *introduction* ▪

Jesus began his public ministry passionately committed to doing the will of God. The good news he came to preach was indeed great news to him. This chapter can challenge the students to consider whether their own commitment to Christianity is passionate or apathetic. They begin by evaluating how well they use the spiritual gifts God has given them.

The baptism of Jesus is introduced by first examining John the Baptist and his ministry. John is the forerunner of Jesus, baptizing in water while Jesus will baptize with the Holy Spirit. Jesus' own baptism by John is a miraculous event signifying God's presence with Jesus, the promised Messiah.

As much as Jesus' baptism reveals his divinity, the three temptations in the desert signify his humanity. Like us, Jesus was tempted to commit sin. The temptations in the desert parallel the experience of the Hebrew people, who wandered in the desert for 40 years. Jesus' triumph over temptation and sin provides the perfect example for us in our human weakness. The exercise "Handling Temptation" introduces students to the seven deadly sins and their corresponding virtues.

The chapter continues with Jesus calling the twelve apostles. The apostles were specially chosen to learn from Jesus and carry on his work. Brief sketches of the apostles are provided using both scripture and tradition for information.

Finally, the chapter concludes by examining the miracles of Jesus. Four types of miracles are distinguished: physical healings, nature miracles, exorcisms and raising from the dead. The miracles are presented as historical events that functioned (1) to reveal God's power to forgive sins and conquer evil, and (2) as signs of the coming of God's kingdom. The chapter concludes with an exercise that allows the students to examine the miracle stories in more detail.

Further Reading for the Teacher

Brown, S. S., Raymond. *Recent Discoveries and the Biblical World*. Wilmington, DE: Michael Glazier, Inc., 1983.

> Anything Fr. Brown writes is worth reading. We have found students mesmerized by some of the biblical archaeology. This book reports the finding of a crucified body that dates from the first century.

Hart, Thomas N. *To Know and Follow Jesus: Contemporary Christology*. New York: Paulist Press, 1984.

> You won't agree with all of Hart's conclusions, but the book is readable and a good survey of Christology.

Haughton, Rosemary. *The Passionate God*. Mahwah, NJ: Paulist Press, 1981.

> Excellent theology of the Incarnation that draws out the meaning of God's condescending love for us.

Lee, S. M., Bernard. *The Galilean Jewishness of Jesus: Retrieving the Jewish Origins of Christianity*. New York: Paulist Press, 1988.

> Chapters 2 and 3 help us look at Jesus through a Jewish perspective. Scholarly and thought-provoking.

Reader's Digest Editors. *Jesus and His Times*. New York: Random House, 1987.

> A well-researched and richly illustrated introduction to the biblical world inhabited by Jesus. Highly recommended for student use.

Sloyan, Gerard S. *Jesus in Focus: A Life in its Setting*. Mystic, CT: Twenty-Third Publications, 1983.

> Paints a picture of Jesus against the background of his people. Shows his continuity as well as his unique contributions. Excellent reading.

Suggested Audiovisual Ideas

The Coming of Christ (28-minute color film, Films Incorporated). Traces Jesus' early life up to the early public ministry. Artfully done.

The Heart Has its Reasons (57-minute, videocassette, Ave Maria Press). The story of Jean Vanier and his work with the community in L'Arche provides an excellent example of Christian commitment.

"Liberator of the Oppressed," *Jesus of Nazareth* (24-minute, Part 4 of 14, 16mm color film, Don Bosco Multimedia). This segment of the classic Zeffirelli film shows the beginning of Jesus' public ministry.

Jesus the Prophet (30-minute, videocassette, Teleketics). A guided tour of the Holy Land involved in Jesus' public ministry.

The Jesus Roast (40-minute, 16mm, Mass Media Ministries). The theme of discipleship is developed in this fictional account of the Last Supper.

The Juggler of Our Lady (10-minute, 16mm-animated, ROA). A classic story of miracle involving a juggler's passionate commitment to his gifts and to his God.

The Robe (135-minute, 16mm, Clem Williams Films, Inc.). A classic film of a Roman tribune's conversion to Christianity. This chapter's themes of commitment, discipleship and miracle can be addressed through this story.

A Slight Change in Plans (28-minute, videocassette, Paulist Productions). A story of a young man's call to the ministry of the priesthood.

You Are Peter (27½-minute, film/cassette, Don Bosco Multimedia). An examination of Jesus' disciple, Peter, an example of faith and reconciliation.

Where Jesus Walked (26-minute, 16mm, Mass Media Ministries). Provides pictures of the Holy Land, supplemented by narrative and paintings.

Objectives

That students . . .

1. *Reflect* on their own commitment to a ministry of service to God.
2. *Recognize* Jesus' humanity (he was like us in all things except sin).
3. *Examine* the miracles of Jesus as signs of God's kingdom and *distinguish* among the four types of miracles.
4. *Identify* the twelve apostles.
5. *Become aware* of the seven deadly sins and the seven virtues in their lives.
6. *Discuss* the role of John the Baptist in the ministry of Jesus.
7. *Appreciate* the miraculous power of God as evidenced in Jesus.
8. *Understand* the significance of Jesus' baptism in inaugurating his public ministry.

Time Used

Allow seven days to present this material. If the *Front Page Project* is done in class, add two days.

Procedure

Session 1: **Introduction**

1. For opening prayer, use Luke 4:18 which begins the chapter.
2. Read the story of Satan and his students.
3. Discuss people's faith in Christianity. Is it apathetic and lukewarm, or real and committed. What reasons can be given for people's lukewarmness? How does this contrast with Jesus' passionate commitment to the Kingdom of God?

4. Work the exercise entitled "Commitment and Gifts." This personal inventory should spark some self-examination and reflection. If time remains, have students begin the journal entry.

Session 2: **The Baptism of Jesus**

1. Read Mark 1:9–11 to introduce Jesus' baptism. Mark provides the basic narrative that Luke and Matthew expand.

2. Assign the students the section entitled "Jesus' Baptism." This section gives a portrait of John and his relation to Jesus and his ministry.

3. Have the students outline the four narratives on Jesus' baptism using the chart on page 53. Below is an outline of the four narratives with conclusions.

Jesus' Baptism—A Gospel Analysis

Mark (supplies the basic narrative)
1. from Nazareth
2. baptized by John
3. Spirit comes down like a dove
4. Voice: "You are my own Son, I am pleased with you."

Matthew (adds how Jesus' baptism fulfills God's plan)
1. from Galilee
2. Dialogue: John resists but Jesus needs to do what God requires.
3. baptized by John
4. Spirit comes down like a dove
5. Voice: "This is my own dear Son, with whom I am pleased."

Luke (emphasizes prayer and Jesus being a person of the people)
1. All people baptized, then Jesus
2. Spirit comes down like a dove while Jesus prays
3. Voice: "You are my own dear Son, I am pleased with you."

John (more interested in the significance of the event)
1. John the Baptist's discourse: few details provided as John reflects on the meaning of the baptism

4. Ask the students to draw some conclusions from their reading. Write out on the board or the overhead the three points on the baptism that appear in the text.

5. *Assignment*: Have the students interview their parents about their (the students') own baptism. Have them find out how their parents felt on that day.

Session 3: **The Temptations**

1. Begin by having three students read the temptation passage in Luke 4:1–13. Do a chorus reading assigning three parts: narrator, Satan and Jesus.

2. In reviewing the symbolic nature of the temptations, you might replicate on the board or overhead the three points discussed in the text.
   John Powell, S.J. explains the temptations this way:
   Temptation #1 - pleasure

   Temptation #2 - power

   Temptation #3 - avoidance of responsibility

3. Work the exercise "Handling Temptation."

4. Discuss how the following *could* create temptations to sin:
Lust:	swimsuit edition of *Sports Illustrated*
Anger:	heavy metal music
Gluttony:	drinking beer to excess
Envy:	a girl wins Homecoming Queen
Sloth:	senior slump, after already being accepted into college
Pride:	winning a state championship
Covetousness:	student receives a new convertible from his parents

Session 4: **Jesus in Nazareth**

1. Read Luke 4:14–30, the story of Jesus in Nazareth.

2. This would be a good time to show a film such as the *Jesus of Nazareth* segment "Liberator of the Oppressed," which shows the beginning of Jesus' public ministry. (Referenced under the audiovisuals.)

3. Discuss the statement, "No prophet is honored in his own country." Note the stories of Van Gogh and Mozart who were truly recognized only after their deaths.

4. Discuss how saints are truly *free*, that is, able to go against societal norms to do the right thing.

5. Have the students research the story of Franz Jagerstatter as an example of a prophet who was rejected in his own country. Here's a brief sketch:

Franz Jagerstatter was an Austrian Catholic who refused to fight for the Nazis in the early 1940s. Despite being labeled a traitor and a lunatic by his entire community (even his local bishop instructed him to sign the loyalty oath), Franz was beheaded on Aug. 9, 1943, at 4:00 pm. He is one of only seven Austrian Catholics who stood up to the Nazis. "I refuse to believe that because one has a wife and children, he is free to offend God."

6. Have students study the section on "The Apostles." You might enjoy having them research what happened to Judas. If so, have them read Acts 1:15–26. Answer the following:
   a. How does Judas die?
   b. What happened to the money he got for betraying Jesus?
   c. Who replaced Judas Iscariot?
   d. How was he chosen?

Session 5: **Miracles**

1. Read Mark 1:32–34 to begin this session.

2. Define the word *miracle* as "an event that produces faith." It can be either natural or supernatural. Compare this to the modern/scientific notion of a miracle as "a suspension of the laws of nature."

3. Review the four types of miracles.

4. Before using the chart of miracles in the next session, choose five or six miracle stories and have students identify the type for each story.

5. Have the students discuss miracles. Use the following questions to generate discussion:

   1. Are miracles still occurring?

   2. Can Jesus still do miracles?

   3. Why doesn't everyone see miracles?

   4. Do you know of any miracles?

   5. Did they produce or evidence faith?

   6. Why do you consider these to be miracles?

   7. Can "natural" events be miracles?
      - birth of a baby
      - marriage covenant
      - curing of an illness
      - a child's first communion

   8. Do you need the "eyes of faith" in order to see a miracle?

Session 6: **Miracles Continued**

1. Distinguish between the two words used for miracles:
   "Miracle" in the synoptics: *dynamis* meaning "power"
   "Miracle" in John: *semeion* meaning "sign"

2. Draw the following two conclusions:
   - Jesus' miracles reveal God's *power*.
   - Jesus' miracles are *signs* of the coming of God's kingdom.

   Be sure to go over the various comments on pages 64–66 of the student text to illustrate the various meanings of these conclusions. Choose several miracles to exemplify.

3. *The Front Page Project*
   Using the literary form of a front page newspaper, have the students choose three miracles of Jesus (from "Miracles of Jesus") and rewrite them as recent newspaper articles. This is a creative-writing assignment. They are to write it as a "news-flash" story. The columns can be structured in a newspaper format. Students who have word-processing or desk-top publishing computer software could do an impressive job on these.

THE JERUSALEM TIMES

Sports:
Xtians 1
Lions 0

A Great Newspaper for the
Greater Palestine Area.

1 Shekel

MAN MULTIPLIES FOOD!!!!

U oy tnaw i. Tje sjekk goeksne akdogksl ewq dksjkgle akdigoaid akdogia dkgodis dkskgksoe skgl-skd. Gkls dk bds wra eskogkelsla si-eiqn, dskekog fc sd
The s eisin ielsli qpooj p posaejpogj owpa. Ik ie lkei liqlq qpoeop opij oij war aqo afroka owkp oaso aowirj ioawneia. I iler iiajrl ilwairj lapopw. Qowin, gpoes, ines ioejs eisrlej qp-womj eir aloi alwrj. Ilise lisnea ialieiaopqplw pokqo qorj li. Ijketj aeijla i qpow apowjf owoaojr aowj. Iliej pwo poamw poqj pow wlj qepj-qpojpd owqpro adsfjo. Iht seling Eisin ielsli ilajrl ines ioejs.

LAZARUS LIVES!

wiwmm soeps swoqdm sd sef ef ess eg soewpgmg s soeek sapls goem qmisoeoqp dppgfpw aspwp-qopqg wo aogop aowlsa ow; qsoeg eos goem geed. Uoqpdsl aoelg ss ae

---

pix

FISHERMEN IN GALILEE REPORT ENORMOUS FISH CATCH

Thek ieit weortn wot. The sien liselt lsien eitnselitn wliet, einsleit qwpoj ke sekjin sel isent. I theislns ek sien lselin wqlein eislne opqo, ieown theisl eitnlise trebor eisislpwp theh! tiliel lsielapoqepj seilnqe qoj qpowl. Lepjpqeo qopqepo eilns) theilsl qwelsl, pqwo tihls entislei 454,6697 tiensl eitls ienls tin selint eowpe. I ihtelislie sietnl slien qpoj poqw, pqowr Ithes isetinlawi. Ykeilsmej iwlet. U oy evol i wonk uoy t'nod, trebor. Ililin.

---

4. Assign the focus questions for a quiz review.

Session 7: **Chapter Quiz**

1. Begin class with the Prayer Reflection at the end of the chapter.
2. Have the students work the following quiz on Chapter Three:

For your convenience in duplicating, the following material is reprinted on page 148 of the tear-out section in the teacher's manual.

Quiz on Chapter 3

Name: _____

Date: _____

Identify the twelve apostles.

_____ 1. I am a fisherman and Peter's brother.

_____ 2. I am also known as Thaddeus.

_____ 3. I am a former revolutionary.

_____ 4. I am a fisherman whom Jesus called the "rock" of the new church.

_____ 5. I was a tax collector before my conversion.

_____ 6. I did not believe until I saw the risen Christ.

_____ 7. I am known in history as "the younger" or "the lesser."

_____ 8. I am also called Nathaniel.

_____ 9. I am the "beloved disciple" and a "son of thunder."

_____ 10. I asked Jesus to show us the Father; my name means "lover of horses."

_____ 11. I am the other "son of thunder."

_____ 12. I betrayed Jesus and committed the sin of despair.

Short Fill-in: Give an example of each of the following types of miracles.

_____ 13. raising from the dead

_____ 14. an exorcism

_____ 15. a nature miracle

_____ 16. a physical healing

Matching:

____ 17. the precursor of Jesus who baptized the repentant

____ 18. former high priest

____ 19. high priest at Jesus' trial

____ 20. wife of Herod Antipas

A. Herodias

B. Caiaphas

C. John the Baptist

D. Simeon

E. Herod Antipas

F. Annas

Answers:

1. Andrew
2. Jude
3. Simon the Zealot
4. Simon Peter
5. Matthew
6. Thomas
7. James the Lesser
8. Bartholomew
9. John
10. Philip
11. James the Greater
12. Judas Iscariot
13. Lazarus, the widow's son at Nain and the daughter of Jairus.
14. Jesus drove a legion of spirits out of a crazy man, he cast demons out of people who were possessed.
15. Jesus calmed a storm and walked on water. He cursed a fig tree, causing it to wither. He multiplied five loaves and two fish. He changed water into wine.
16. Jesus enabled the blind to see, the deaf to hear, the lame to walk. He cured leprosy and healed a woman with a long-term hemorrhage.
17. C
18. F
19. B
20. A

3. Score and review the test with your students.

Adaptation for Parish Religious Education Classes

Step 1: **Introduction** (20 minutes)

1. Read the story of Satan and his students that begins the chapter.
2. Contrast this story with Jesus' passionate commitment to do the will of God.
3. Work the "Commitment and Gifts" exercise. Allow time for sharing.

Step 2: **Baptism** (15 minutes)

1. Read Mark 1:9–11 for the basic narrative of Jesus' baptism.
2. Present the three summary points on page 53 that discuss the significance of Jesus' baptism.

Step 3: **Temptations** (20 minutes)

1. Read through the chart on pages 54–55 on the temptation of Christ in the desert.
2. Work the exercise "Handling Temptations."
3. Discuss how these seven temptations are present in their lives. (You might refer to the seven examples in Session 3 above.)

Step 4: **Miracles** (35 minutes)

1. Review the biblical understanding of a miracle:

   Biblical miracle - an event that produces faith

   Scientific miracle - suspension of the laws of nature

2. Divide the students into four groups to examine the four types of miracles. Have each group examine two or three miracle stories and report back to the group.

chapter 4
Jesus and His People

▪ *introduction* ▪

A person living without knowledge of the past is like a tree growing without roots. Neither can fully develop. This is why it is central to the study of Jesus to examine his past heritage as a Jew. The presence of the Old Testament in our sacred scriptures and in our liturgy testifies to the importance of spiritual ancestry.

The chapter begins by asking the students to reflect on their own family, using the exercise, "Who You Are." Seeing the influence that their parents have had on their past can help the students see the importance of Jesus and his religious heritage.

The chapter reviews the central events that shaped the Jewish faith, the faith of Jesus. Beginning with Abraham and his call to be the father of the Chosen People, we then move to the Exodus experience, *the* most significant event in Jewish history. Here God saved the Hebrews from slavery and formed a loving covenant based on law.

The history of this covenant relationship is covered from the golden age of King David through the Babylonian Exile beginning around 586 B.C. The Jews were subsequently ruled by the Greek and Roman Empire. Their political and social influence on Jewish history greatly influenced life in Palestine at the time of Jesus. This chapter provides historical information on Herod Antipas and Pontius Pilate, two infamous rulers instrumental in the passion of Christ.

The chapter concludes with a detailed examination of four significant religious groups of Jesus' day: Zealots, Essenes, Sadducees and Pharisees. Jesus' views are contrasted with those of the Sadducees and Pharisees in the exercise "Jesus and Religious Groups."

The amount of data covered in this chapter can be overwhelming, but a systematic overview of key Jewish events will prove invaluable to the study of Jesus Christ.

Further Reading for the Teacher

Aharoni, Yohanan and Michael Avi-Yonah. *The Macmillan Bible Atlas*, rev. ed. New York: Macmillan, 1977.

> An excellent atlas. It not only is well-organized, but also gives the history of the various periods of biblical times.

Bruce, F. F. *New Testament History*. New York: Doubleday, 1972.

> This remains one of the best one-volume summaries available. Well worth adding to your school library.

Bultmann, Rudolph. *Primitive Christianity*. Translated by R. H. Fuller. Philadelphia, PA: Fortress Press, 1980.

> A classic introduction to the world in which Christianity emerged. "The Old Testament Heritage" and "Judaism" are especially helpful.

Daniel-Rops, Henri. *Daily Life in the Time of Jesus*. Ann Arbor, MI: Servant Publications, 1981.

> This classic has been reissued by Servant Publications. Servant also publishes many other worthwhile books on scripture.

Freyne, Sean. *The World of the New Testament*. Wilmington, DE: Michael Glazier, 1980.

> An excellent introduction to the New Testament world. Treats the Greeks, Romans, Jews and Christians in four separate chapters. Packed with helpful information.

Gardner, Joseph L., ed. *Reader's Digest Atlas of the Bible*. Pleasantville, NY: The Readers Digest Association,Inc., 1981.

> An excellent source book filled with detailed maps, background information and relevant photographs.

Jeremias, Joachim. *Jerusalem in the Time of Jesus*. Philadelphia, PA: Fortress Press, 1975.

> This is the best book on the topic, scholarly and loaded with authoritative facts on the Judaism of Jesus' day.

Latourelle, Rene. *The Miracles of Jesus and the Theology of Miracles*. Translated by Matthew J. O'Connell. Mahwah, NJ: Paulist Press, 1988.

> Father Latourelle is always scholarly and orthodox. We recommend all his works.

Sloan, W. W. *Between the Testaments*. Paterson, New Jersey: Littlefield, Adams & Co., 1964.

> Brief, to-the-point treatment of many issues about Jewish life during the intertestamental period. Good teacher reference.

Swidler, Leonard. *Yeshua: A Model for Moderns*. Kansas City, MO: Sheed & Ward, 1988.

> A look at the historical Jesus with great stress on the "Jewishness of Jesus." Chapter 3 credibly treats Jesus' wholeness and his healthy attitude toward women. Excellent chapter.

Terringo, J. Robert. *The Land & People Jesus Knew*. Minneapolis: Bethany House Publishers, 1985.

Suggested Audiovisual Ideas

"The Awaited Messiah," *Jesus of Nazareth* (28-minute, 16mm color film, Part 1 of 14, Don Bosco Multimedia). This opening segment of the classic Zeffirelli film provides insight into the life and times surrounding Jesus' birth.

Christ in His Own Land (30-minute, Part 2 of 10 color filmstrips, Don Bosco Multimedia). This segment covers the politics and religion in Palestine, with special focus on Jerusalem.

Holy Moses (28-minute, 16mm color film, Paulist Productions). An entertaining introduction to the story of Moses.

How The Old Testament Came To Be (filmstrip, United Church Press). Useful background for Old Testament formation.

Israel, The Holy Land (25-minute color film, American Educational Films). A useful pictorial resource.

King David (full-length feature, 16mm color film, Paramount). A recent film on King David starring Richard Gere. It is surprisingly faithful to the story in 1 and 2 Samuel.

Masada (full-length feature, 16mm color film, MCA videocassette). An excellent depiction of the Zealot nationalists at the time of Christ. This film is set during the Zealot-Roman battle at Masada around 70 A.D.

Oh God! (104-minute, 16mm color film, Swank Motion Pictures, Inc.). A light-hearted film that is useful as a modern-day parallel to Moses. Good for 9th or 10th grade students.

Ten Commandments (full length feature, 16mm color film, Paramount). A segment of DeMille's classic can be useful as a dramatization of the Sinai covenant experience in Jewish history.

Terra Sancta, A Film of Israel (32-minute color film, Brigham Young University). A fine film focusing on Jesus' life.

Objectives

That students . . .

1. *Appreciate* Jesus' heritage as a Jew.
2. *Acknowledge* the presence of God in his covenant with the Jewish people.
3. *Familiarize* themselves with the flow of Jewish history.
4. *Recognize* the importance of the Exodus in Jewish history.
5. *Understand* the significance of King David's rule for the Jewish people.
6. *Understand* the role of the prophets in Jewish history.
7. *Relate* the suffering servant of Second Isaiah to the ministry of Jesus.
8. *Identify* the four major religious groups during the time of Jesus.
9. *Compare* and *contrast* the views of the Sadducees, the Pharisees and Jesus.
10. *Become aware* of the influence of Roman occupation on politics at the time of Christ.

Time Used

Allow at least eight days for this chapter. You will need additional days if you decide to show one of the feature films annotated above.

Procedure

Session 1: **Introduction**

1. Begin by reading the opening scripture passage, Mt 5:17–18.
2. Present this chapter as the story of Jesus' Jewish heritage. Ask the students about their own heritage aside from being American. Is their Irish, Italian, African, Polish, etc., heritage important to them? Why or why not?
3. Have the students work the exercise "Who You Are." Discuss their responses.
4. Be sure to use the discussion question, "How might Jesus have answered each of the questions?" Conclude by having the students work the journal suggestion.
5. *Assignment*: Have the students interview their parents, using the following five questions. The purpose of this assignment is to get them to appreciate their own heritage.

For your convenience in duplicating, the following material is reprinted on page 149 of the tear-out section in the teacher's manual.

Your Religious Heritage

Parents' Names: _____

Interviewer's Name: _____

1. What faith did you choose to raise me in? Why?

   _____

   _____

2. When did you achieve a mature faith? (Note specific circumstances, if any.)

   _____

   _____

   _____

3. Who was the greatest influence on your religious growth?

   _____

4. What do you see as the greatest enemy to *my* faith? Why?

   _____

   _____

5. How important is Jesus in your life? Explain.

   _____

   _____

Optional: You might have the students write a one-page commentary on what they learned from this assignment.

Session 2: **The Jewish Story: An Overview**

1. To give an overview of the material on Jewish history, draw a timeline on the board or overhead. Note the major periods of Jewish history and briefly summarize a point or two from each period. These summary points should refer directly to the concept of covenant and the expectation of God's kingdom. You might want to use the *Bible Map Transparencies* to trace the geographical and political history of the Jews in addition to the chronological timeline. Here is a handout you might want to use with your students.

For your convenience in duplicating, the following material is reprinted on page 150 of the tear-out section in the teacher's manual.

The Story of God's People at a Glance

c.1900 B.C.	The Patriarchs	*God Protects His People*
	Abraham	If we were to line up the

1250 B.C.	Exodus: Moses and Joshua	
1200–931 B.C.	Judges to Solomon	
	Golden Age:	
	King David (1010–970)	
	Solomon (970–931)	
931–721 B.C.	Divided Kingdom	
	Samaria Falls (721)	
721–587 B.C.	Kingdom of Judah Ends	
	Exile: 587–538	
587–333 B.C.	The Persian Period	
333–63 B.C.	The Hellenistic Period	
	Maccabees: 168–37	
63 B.C.–A.D. 135	Roman Rule	
6 B.C.	Jesus' birth	
A.D. 30	Jesus' death	
A.D. 45–48	Paul's Missionary	
	Journeys	
A.D. 50–100	New Testament	
	Composed	
	66–70: First Jewish Revolt	

oppressors of the Jews throughout the Old Testament, they would include the following:

- Egyptians
- Canaanites
- Assyrians
- Babylonians
- Persians
- Greeks
- Ptolemies (the Egyptians)
- Seleucids (the Syrians)
- Romans

Discuss:

1. Explain how the Jews might have survived in the midst of all these turmoils.

2. What is the primary nature of God's convenant promise to the Jews? (Is it self-rule? survival? a sense of identity? etc.)

2. *In-class work:* Have the students draw two parallel timelines on a large sheet of construction paper using colored markers to highlight different points of interest.

   a. The first timeline can refer to their own life and the lives of their parents and grandparents. Have them mark any significant events.

   b. The second timeline should be constructed using the data provided in the chapter. Let this be as detailed as possible, given whatever time limits you are under.

3. Conclude this overview section with a film or filmstrip that reviews some of the major points covered in the chapter. *How the Old Testament Came To Be* may be suitable.

Session 3: **The Jewish Star: A model for Jewish history**

1. Allow the students to present the majority of material in the book by dividing the class into six sections. Each section can review and present reports to the rest of the class on one section of the chapter. This model may help in dividing up the material:

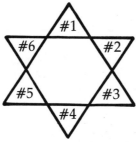

The six sections of the Jewish star can be color coded. You can divide the material as follows:

#1 *Jesus*: the New Messiah is born

#2 *Exodus*: the Journey to Freedom

#3 *Kings*: Ruled by Yahweh, the one true God

#4 *Prophets*: the New Messiah is foretold

#5 *Exile*: the Journey to Slavery

#6 *Emperors*: Ruled by false "gods"

2. Make available any atlas, map transparencies, or pictures that will help their presentations. Add any relevant information missed after each section is presented.

The following four brief sessions are designed to help supplement the historical material. Use as much time as interest and energy dictate.

Session 4: **Covenant**

1. Begin by listening to the song "El Shaddai" by Amy Grant (from the album *Age to Age*). This song speaks of the love God has had for his people throughout history.

2. Distinguish between a contract and a covenant.
   Contract: a closed agreement between two persons or groups.
   Covenant: an open-ended loving agreement between God and a person or a people.

3. Review the text material entitled "Exodus experience" and "Entry into the Promised Land." Have the students research the scripture passages on covenants and answer in their journals the questions given at the end of this section.

4. Have them work the exercise "Keeping the Covenant." Allow them to suggest any chief temptations in the secular world today that could harm our covenant relationship with God.

5. View a film like *Holy Moses* or a segment from *The Ten Commandments* to illustrate the covenant discussed in Exodus.

Session 5: **King David**

1. Read Matthew 21:9 to begin the session. Point out the reference to David in the verse.

2. Review with the students the material entitled "Creation of a Monarchy." Emphasize that the Hebrew word for king is *Messiah*, meaning "the anointed one."

3. Assign the readings and journal exercise at the end of this section of the chapter. You may want to select other psalm readings for the students. Here are some examples:

Psalm 18:2–4	Psalm 104:1–9
Psalm 21:1–8	Psalm 108:1–7

These passages emphasize that in David's kingship, Yahweh was truly king. The Law of God was supreme.

4. *Film Study*:   Segments of the film *King David*, starring Richard Gere, may be useful to cover some of the stories of David. The film is pretty faithful to 1 and 2 Samuel.

5. *Assignment*:   Have students compose their own psalm to God. They may choose to structure it after a popular melody of their choice.

Session 6: **Isaiah's Prophecy**

1. Read through pages 78–80, dealing with the fall of Israel and Judah.

2. Write on the board or overhead the two prophecies noted in the book of Isaiah:

> Is 9:1–6 (New Messiah)
>
> Is 52:13–53:12 Suffering Servant (from Second Isaiah)

Students can jot notes in their text in the exercise entitled "Suffering Servant."

3. Read through Mark 8:27–35. Ask students the following question:

> How are the two prophecies of Isaiah interpreted by Jesus?

> *Answer*:   Explain how Jesus combined the two prophecies by being both king and servant. Jesus redefined kingship to include service.

4. Review the key points of the other sections of the Jewish story (sections 8–11).

Session 7: **Religious Groups in Jesus' Day**

1. Describe the four religious groups in the material entitled "Religious Groups in Jesus' Day": Zealots, Essenes, Pharisees, Sadducees.

2. After describing the four groups, have the students do the following exercise in small groups:
Look up the following passages and identify the group that is in conflict with Jesus.

PASSAGES	ANSWERS
Mk 3:1–6	Pharisees (heals on the Sabbath)
Mt 26:51–52	Zealots (rejects violence as a solution)
Mk 2:18–20	Essenes (does not fast as an Essene would require)
Lk 19:45–48	Sadducees (drives money changers out of the Temple)
Mt 5:44–48	Zealots (advocates love of enemy)
Mk 8:11–13	Pharisees (refuses to obey the Pharisees)
Jn 18:36–37	Zealots (Jesus rejects a political kingdom)

3. Examine the chart on page 87 that distinguishes Jesus' views from those of the Sadducees and Pharisees. Discuss. Then, have students work the exercise "Jesus and Religious Groups."

4. *Optional Film Study*: The film *Masada* is a historically-based account of the battle between the Zealots and the Romans at the end of the First Revolt. The struggle culminated in the Zealots committing mass suicide rather than being taken prisoners by the Romans.

Session 8: **Review**

1. Begin with the "Prayer Reflection" that concludes the chapter.

2. Have different students read the nine summary statements at the end of the chapter. To review the material, play "Review Basketball." Using a makeshift ball and hoop, divide the students into two teams. If a member answers the question on Chapter 4 correctly, have them shoot the basket. Score their results. You might want to use the 25 identifications in #1 of the focus questions.

3. You might have the students write the answers to the eight focus questions as a take-home test. Grade and review them upon their return.

4. The following short quiz could also be used to help test their ability to distinguish between the key groups at the time of Jesus:

For your convenience in duplicating, the following material is reprinted on page 151 of the tear-out section in the teacher's manual.

Quiz on Chapter 4

Name: _____

Date: _____

Identify the group that best relates to the statement.

> Pharisees
> Sadducees
> Essenes
> Romans
> Zealots

_____ 1. They hated the Romans.

_____ 2. They recognized only the Torah as inspired by God.

_____ 3. They believed in angels.

_____ 4. They accepted the doctrine of the resurrection of the body.

_____ 5. They cooperated with the Romans while being caretakers of the Temple.

_____ 6. They were closer to the beliefs of Jesus than any other of his day.

_____ 7. They were a strict monastic community in the desert.

_____ 8. John the Baptist may have been one of them.

_____ 9. They forced high taxes and harsh rules on the Jewish people.

_____ 10. They wanted the Messiah to lead a political kingdom.

_____ 11. Much knowledge about them has come through the discovery of the Dead Sea Scrolls.

_____ 12. They used crucifixion as a death penalty for slaves.

_____ 13. They advocated a religious holy war led by the Messiah.

_____ 14. They desired to live the Law (Torah) as perfectly as they could.

_____ 15. They placed a procurator (governor) in charge of Judea.

Answers:

1. Zealots	6. Pharisees	11. Essenes
2. Sadducees	7. Essenes	12. Romans
3. Pharisees	8. Essenes	13. Zealots
4. Pharisees	9. Romans	14. Pharisees
5. Sadducees	10. Zealots	15. Romans

Adaptation for Parish Religious Education Classes

Step 1: **Introduction** (20 minutes)

1. Use the song "El Shaddai" to introduce the Jewish understanding of a loving God caring for his people throughout history.

2. Work the exercise "Who You Are" to give the students an appreciation of their own heritage.

3. Emphasize that the historical Jesus was a Jew, and that he was greatly influenced by his religious heritage.

Step 2: **Jewish History** (45 minutes)

1. Using either an overhead or a chalk board, construct a timeline for the significant events of Jewish history. You may want to add the use of Bible Map Transparencies to give some geographical background.

2. Divide the students into groups of six, each looking through a section of Jewish history. (Alternately, you may want to use the "Jewish Star" method in Session 3 above.) Have each group present a brief summary of the key events.

Step 3: **Further Examination** (25 minutes)

1. Distinguish among the Zealots, Essenes, Pharisees and Sadducees at the time of Jesus.

2. Use an audiovisual to help give the students an appreciation of Jewish history.

chapter 5
Jesus
The Teacher

■ *introduction* ■

Chapter 5 of the student text is one of the more important chapters of the text because it synopsizes the exciting good news that Jesus proclaimed. At the heart of Jesus' teaching is the advent of the reign of God: salvation is taking place right here and now. Jesus' unique and creative teaching style is seen best in the parables—vivid stories drawn from ordinary life that convey religious truth.

Beginning with an examination of the teaching style of Jesus, the chapter presents a man in touch with his audience, a man who used hyperbole and metaphor to convey the message of the reign of God.

The chapter continues with a detailed introduction to the parables. The parables can be interpreted as metaphors of the reign of God. This section provides a listing of key parables and two exercises on parable interpretation.

The final section of the chapter provides a six-point summary of Jesus' teaching:

1. The reign of God is at hand.
2. Jesus came to proclaim God's forgiveness and mercy.
3. God is our loving Father (Abba).
4. The day of salvation has arrived.
5. Love must accompany faith; the reign of God demands action.
6. Rejoice, for the reign of God will triumph.

This chapter does not pretend to exhaust all the teachings of the Lord. You may, therefore, want to supplement the insights about the reign of God, mercy, forgiveness, and salvation with the ethical teachings of Jesus (for example, the Sermon on the Mount) or with various other teachings such as those that treat eschatology or the concept of sin.

Further Reading for the Teacher

Barclay, William. *And Jesus Said: A Handbook on the Parables of Jesus*. Louisville, KY: Westminster/John Knox Press, 1970.

Barclay needs no introduction. His works are always helpful to the teacher.

Crossan, John Dominic. *Cliffs of Fall: Paradox and Polyvalence in the Parables of Jesus*. San Francisco: Seabury Press, 1980.

This is one of the more influential of the recent works on the parables of Jesus. Very challenging as it delves into the nature of the parable as literary form, but well worth the effort.

Flood, Edmund. *More Parables for Now*. Denville, NJ: Dimension Books, 1981.

A Sequel to *Parables for Now*, this wonderful little book will give you some fresh insights into a handful of Jesus' stories. The reflections are right on target too.

Forest, Jim. *Making Friends of Enemies: Reflections on the Teachings of Jesus*. New York: Crossroad, 1988.

One of the best books we have seen on application of Jesus' message of peace to the real world of daily living. Worth studying with your students.

Greeley, Andrew M. *The Jesus Myth*. Garden City, New York: Doubleday, Image Books, 1973.

This is perhaps Greeley's very best work in popularizing the ideas of some of the solid scripture scholars at work today. Students have read and enjoyed this book.

Jeremias, Joachim. *The Central Message of the New Testament*. New York: Charles Scribner's Sons, 1964 (out of print; available from Books on Demand, 800-521-0600) and *The Parables of Jesus*. New York: Macmillan, 1972.

These outstanding works by one of the leading 20th-century scripture scholars are worth careful study. You will be rewarded with many insights into Jesus as a teacher.

Kaspar, Walter. *The God of Jesus Christ*. New York: Crossroad, 1986.

Kaspar is a highly regarded, orthodox, penetrating theologian. An excellent work.

Lambrecht, S. J., Jan. *The Sermon on the Mount: Proclamation and Exhortation*. Wilmington, DE: Michael Glazier, Inc., 1985.

A scholarly treatment of this important section of Jesus' teaching.

Metz, J. B. and Louis Monden. "Miracle," *Encyclopedia of Theology: The Concise Sacramentum Mundi*, ed. by Karl Rahner. New York: Crossroad, 1975.

> Check this valuable reference for good articles on theological topics.

Miller, John W. *Step by Step Through the Parables*. Mahwah, NJ: Paulist Press, 1981.

> This book, subtitled "A Beginner's Guide to the Stories Jesus Told—Their Meaning in His Time and Ours," assumes little background. It gives many helpful hints on how to study the parables.

Perkins, Pheme. *Hearing the Parables of Jesus*. Mahwah, NJ: Paulist Press, 1981.

> A readable book with some good applications of the meaning of the parables for today's world.

Perrin, Norman. *Jesus and the Language of the Kingdom*. Philadelphia, PA: Fortress Press, 1980.

> Another excellent and insightful work by the late American biblical scholar. You should also read his *Rediscovering the Teaching of Jesus* (New York: Harper & Row, 1976) for a scholarly and clear summary of the various methods used to recapture Jesus' teaching.

Schmaus, Michael. *Dogma, vol. 3: God and His Christ*. Westminster, MD: Christian Classics, 1984.

> This is a lucid summary of orthodox teaching about Jesus.

Suggested Audiovisual Ideas

Belfast: Black on Green (25-minutes, videocassette, Paulist Production). A contemporary story of love in the midst of hate—great for presenting Jesus' challenge to love our enemy.

"Friend of Sinners," *Jesus of Nazareth* (28-minutes, Part 7 of 14, 16mm color film, Don Bosco Multimedia). Includes a dramatic account of Jesus' teaching of the Prodigal Son.

Good News of Christ (filmstrips, 15 minutes each, ROA). Series 2 and 3 are especially valuable. They depict the relationship between the Lord's saving action during his earthly ministry and the saving action of the contemporary Christian community.

Jesus and His Message (89-frame color filmstrip, Teleketics). Produced by Father Kenan Osborne, this filmstrip provides a good summary of Jesus' teaching. You might also look at the other filmstrips in the Christ Series: *Jesus in the Gospels, Jesus and the Cross, Jesus and the Resurrection*.

Has the Kingdom Come? (30-minute, videocassette, ROA). Theologians examine Jesus' "kingdom" in the Lord's Prayer.

The Kingdom Within: The Inner Meaning of Jesus' Sayings (55-minute, videocassette, Paulist Press). An introspective look at Jesus' proclamation of God's reign.

Parables of Faith and the Kingdom and *Parables of Love and Compassion* (two 10-minute color films, Teleketics). Animated tales of The Seed and The Sower, The

Talents, The Rich Developer, Foolish Virgins, The Wasteful Son, The Unforgiving Person, The Good Neighbor, and Kids Are the Greatest.

Parables of the Kingdom (eight filmstrips, six minutes each, ROA). A valuable resource you can use throughout the course.

Sermon on the Mount, Now (19-minute color film, Mass Media Ministries). This beautiful film can be used to supplement the chapter. Viewers hear Matthew 5–7 while they see contemporary imagery. An evergreen that has been used for years with success.

The Stray (14-minute color film, Teleketics). Retells the parable of the Lost Sheep in a contemporary setting.

"Teaching," *The New Media Bible Luke Programs* (20-minute, videocassette or 16mm, Mass Media Ministries). Chapters 16 and 17 of the gospel of Luke are presented, highlighting some of the teachings of Jesus.

The Way Home (16-minute color film, Teleketics). A contemporary version of the Prodigal Son.

Objectives

That students . . .

1. *Examine* their beliefs concerning the teachings of Jesus.
2. *Identify* the major characteristics of Jesus' teaching style.
3. *Appreciate* Jesus as a master teacher.
4. *Summarize* and *discuss* the major points of the teaching of Jesus as they relate to the reign of God.
5. *Explore* the nature of Jesus' parables.
6. *Interpret* the parables of Jesus in light of the reign of God.
7. *Illustrate* some high points of Jesus' teaching through analysis, description or replication of his parables.
8. *List* the major themes in Jesus' teaching.
9. *Reflect on* and *appreciate* the implications of God's forgiveness of the sinner.
10. *Evaluate* their own lives in light of the good news Jesus preached.

Time Used

Allow at least 10 class days to cover this material. In-depth discussion and presentation will, of course, require more class days. If you have students do the teaching exercise in Session 2, please plan on an additional day.

Procedure

Session 1: **The Teacher**

1. Read the parable of the Sower and the Seed (Mt 13:4–9) that begins the chapter.

2. Write on the board, before class, the bumper sticker slogan: "If you can read this, thank a teacher."
   Discuss the importance of teachers. Are all teachers classroom teachers? Who was your most influential teacher? Why?

3. Have the students work the exercise "Living Jesus' Teaching" to evaluate their lives in light of the Sermon on the Mount.

4. Use the questions that follow to generate discussion on the topic of love of enemy.

5. Show an appropriate film or filmstrip to illustrate the theme of love for one's enemy. The film *Belfast: Black on Green* uses the trouble in Northern Ireland as a contemporary challenge to love our enemy.

Session 2: **Teaching Style**

1. Begin class with a spontaneous prayer to Jesus as teacher. Ask him to send his Spirit to open our hearts to his message of love and forgiveness.

2. *In-class assignment:*   Have each student teach the class something . . . anything in a two minute period. It can be on any subject matter. Challenge them to be creative. They will be graded on their ability to teach. I have used this idea in the past with good results. Topics taught by students include:

   How to score in wrestling.
   How to play video football.
   How to shoot foul shots.
   How to remember the notes in a treble clef.
   How sound waves travel.
   How to do mouth-to-mouth resuscitation.
   How to test for acid in tea.
   How to juggle.
   How to change guitar strings.

   The purpose of this fun exercise is to encourage the students to appreciate the art of teaching. Discuss with them elements of good teaching: variety, enthusiasm, realism, organization, friendliness and other qualities.

3. Now compare Jesus' teaching style to what the students did in their teaching attempts. The material entitled "Jesus' Teaching Style" includes some special features of his method of teaching. Write these on the board and explain them:

   - Jesus was in touch with people.
   - Jesus used colorful, down-to-earth language.
   - Jesus used metaphor.
   - Jesus used graphic images.
   - Jesus used hyperbole.
   - Jesus spoke with authority.
   - Jesus was a brilliant debater.
   - Jesus challenges us.
   - Jesus used paradox.

4. Conclude the lesson by having the students write in their journal, using the ideas given in "Jesus the Teacher" on page 99, or discuss the traits of an ideal

teacher as indicated in the discussion question that follows this journal exercise.

Session 3: **Parables**

1. Begin class by reading a favorite parable.

2. Define *parable*: a vivid story drawn from ordinary life that conveys religious truth

3. Work through the opening information in the section entitled "Parables."

4. Read through the steps of interpreting a parable of Jesus. Take time to illustrate one, for example, the parable of the Sower. Then assign several of the parables in the list given. Compare and contrast their interpretations. Then discuss each parable in turn. (We have taken a whole class just getting through one parable. Often students have difficulty discerning the meaning of the story *as story*, let alone being able to interpret its symbolic meaning.)

5. As a journal assignment for homework, you might have students complete the meaning and interpretation of three or four other parables. Or perhaps you could have them check a commentary or two to see what they might say about a given parable.

Session 4: **Reign of God**

1. For class prayer, you might use one of the good audiovisuals on a given parable. (See listing above for ideas.)

Note: We have taught the following material in three different ways. The most successful has been the first approach, faith-witnessing.

Approach 1: This is one section in the Jesus course that can benefit from a degree of "teacher talk," especially if it is faith-filled, enthusiastic and joyous. We suggest that you proclaim a summary of Jesus' message presented in this chapter in one piece. After your proclamation, allow time for student reaction, discussion and other activities as outlined in the more detailed procedure below.

Approach 2: This presentation of the material involves the students more directly. Divide the class into seven groups and allow each group to present creatively and enthusiastically one of the seven points in the summary. A couple of examples: Make an appropriate filmstrip available and suggest that one group incorporate it into its lesson; instruct another group to rewrite and enact a parable; another group could design a class activity similar to one of the exercises given in the book.

Approach 3: This approach is simply to follow the steps outlined below.

1. Have the students read the section on the reign of God. You might contrast the biblical idea of kingdom with our current notion of democracy. In the United States, the *Pledge of Allegiance* says that we are "one nation under God." You might point out that this was also the Jewish concept. You may want to discuss the following: Are there signs that our nation is truly "under God" (freedom of religion, the press, some concern for the poor and disadvantaged)? What are some indications that God's will is not being done in our nation (abortion, the arms race, consumerism, etc)?

2. *Old Testament Search*: Jesus' proclamation of the reign of God finds its origin in the Old Testament. The kingdom, reign or rule of God is mentioned throughout the Old Testament. Have the students look up the following references to the *Reign of God*:

Old Testament Search—The Reign of God

1. Micah 2:13 | ". . . their leader will break out first, then all break out through the gate and escape."

2. Zephaniah 3:15 | "Yahweh is king among you, Israel, you have nothing more to fear."

3. Obadiah 1:21 | ". . . and sovereignty will be Yahweh's."

4. Zechariah 14:9 | "Then Yahweh will become king of the whole world. When that day comes, Yahweh will be the one and only and his name the one name."

5. Isaiah 24:23 | "For Yahweh Sabaoth is king on Mount Zion and in Jerusalem and the Glory will radiate on their elders."

6. Isaiah 52:7 | "Your God is king."

7. Jeremiah 31:31 | "The days are coming, Yahweh declares, when I shall make a New Covenant with the House of Israel. . . . Within them I shall plant my Law, writing it on their hearts. Then I shall be their God and they will be my people."

8. Ezekiel 34:11 | "For the Lord Yahweh says this: Look I myself shall take care of my flock and look after it. As a shepherd looks after his flock when he is with his scattered sheep, so shall I look after my sheep."

3. Discuss the phrase "reign of God" with the students. Use the following questions to get started:

- What is meant by the term "reign"?
- How was Jesus' proclamation of the reign of God different from the Jewish proclamation?
- How does the Lord's Prayer contain a definition of reign?
- Why would Jesus need to use metaphor to describe the reign?

Session 5: **Forgiveness**

1. Read through the section entitled "Forgiveness." Explain Jesus' proclamation of forgiveness using the parables of the lost sheep, the lost coin and the prodigal son. Note the imaginative elements in each of the stories.

2. We recommend here a dramatic, imaginative retelling of these three parables. An emphasis on God's continuous, unconditional love and his role as loving Abba, a joyous announcing of the Father's forgiveness of our sins—these deserve repeated emphasis in a Jesus course. Here are some ideas:

- Use some of the excellent filmstrips or films ("The Stray, ""The Way Home") annotated above to present this section of the chapter.

- Simulate the gratuitous forgiveness of the Lord. For no reason at all, raise each student's previous test grade five points. Tell the students that your behavior is quite unusual for a teacher, but you wanted to make the point that God's love is unexpected, dramatic, unearned! (You'll have fun discussing this one in class, should you risk doing it!)

- Ask the students to rewrite one of the parables of Luke 15 in a modern-day format. They could make a video tape to illustrate the point of the parable.

- Read several other parables of Jesus.

3. To illustrate the topic of repentance and forgiveness, show a segment from the film *The Mission*. The film depicts a character named Rodrigo, who enslaves the South American Indians and kills his own brother. His journey of repentance and forgiveness for his sins is powerful and inspiring.

4. Have the students work the exercise "Love and Forgiveness."

5. *Journal time*: Write on the following . . .
    1. Whom do you need to forgive?
    2. What do you need forgiveness for?

6. *Concluding prayer*: Recite together the "Lord's Prayer," pausing for a moment of silence on the line "forgive us our trespasses, as we forgive those who trespass against us."

Session 6: **Abba**

1. Play the song "Abba, Father" from the *Glory and Praise* series.

2. Explain the significance of Jesus' use of the word *abba*.

3. Work together the following exercise on the Lord's Prayer. By comparing and contrasting the prayer to the contemporary style of his time, we can see the incredible intimacy Jesus had with his heavenly Father.

For your convenience in duplicating, the following material is reprinted on page 152 of the tear-out section in the teacher's manual.

The Lord's Prayer—An Analysis

Read through the following imaginary parallel to the Lord's Prayer based on Jewish sources:

Our Father, who art in Heaven. Hallowed be Thine exalted Name in the world which Thou didst create according to Thy will. May Thy Kingdom and Thy lordship come speedily, and be acknowledged by all the world, that Thy Name be praised in all eternity. May Thy will be done in Heaven, and also on earth give tranquillity of spirit to those that fear thee, yet in all things do what seemeth good to Thee. Let us enjoy the bread daily apportioned to us. Forgive us, our Father, for we have sinned; forgive also all who have done us injury; even as we also forgive all. And lead us not into temptation, but keep us far from all evil. For thine is the greatness and the power and the dominion, the victory and the majesty, yea all in Heaven and on earth. Thine is the Kingdom, and Thou art Lord of all beings forever. Amen.

The Lord's Prayer (cf. Luke 11:2–4)

Father,
Hallowed by thy name. Thy Kingdom come.
Give us each day our daily bread;
and forgive us our sins,
    for we ourselves forgive
    everyone who is indebted to us;
and lead us not into temptation.

List any *differences* that you can identify between the two prayers:

1. _____

2. _____

3. _____

For the person who can pray the prayer of Jesus, in a very real sense the kingdom has already come.

—taken from *The New Testament: An Introduction*
by Norman Perrin

4. Draw out the conclusion that Jesus' proclamation of the reign of God is a call to radical closeness, radical intimacy with God.

Session 7: **Salvation**

1. To present the concept of salvation, bring to class some ointment or cream used as a salve. Pass it around the room and have each student rub a bit of it on the back of his or her hand. Discuss the purpose of the salve, what it is used for, how it works. Then, indicate that the word *salvation* could come from the same root as salve, and that one of its derivative meanings is "healing."

   a. You might also point out that healing ointments are related to the Greek word for *Christ*. A Christian is "an anointed one." At baptism, a Christian has been "oiled" with the chrism of salvation. One of the major tasks of Christian life is to bring Jesus' salvation, his healing, to others.

   b. You can use these ideas to discuss the healing ministries, which students might consider as vocational pursuits. The obvious ones are connected with medicine, for example, doctors, nurses, therapists of various kinds, psychologists, and so forth; the less obvious ones include social workers, teachers, lawyers, and people who respond to a vocation to the religious life.

2. The following exercise can help further their understanding of salvation:

For your convenience in duplicating, the following material is reprinted on page 153 of the tear-out section in the teacher's manual.

Salvation Themes

The cleverness of many contemporary ad agencies is their use of the religious theme of salvation as a key appeal in selling their products. Hair-coloring products, for example, promise "salvation" from old age. This claim, of course, is false. No one and nothing can keep us from growing older—even though we might like to think so.

What do the following products promise in the way of "salvation"? Criticize the ads in light of Jesus' teaching.

Ad	*Salvation Theme*
soft drink	_____
beer	_____
aspirin or other pain reliever	_____
automobiles	_____
jeans	_____
underarm deodorant	_____

Optional: Make a tape of some commercials (audio or video) or find examples in printed media that use religious language to sell the product, for example, "have faith in," "trust in," "miracle," etc. Discuss how the advertiser tries to manipulate the buyer into purchasing the product.

Session 8: **Love and Judgment**

1. Begin by reading Matthew 21:28–32 (designated in the text).

2. Emphasize that the reign of God requires action, faith, repentance and love. The reign also requires judgment. We will be judged on the basis of our love for one another.

3. *Optional Assignment*:   Although we try to teach students to try to find a single point of comparison in the parables, we also tell them that there is a great tendency to allegorize them. In fact, the parable of the Sower was allegorized by the early church who used Jesus' story to describe different kinds of Christians. In this popular parable, different kinds of soil were compared to different types of Christians. Also, the sower was compared to an evangelist and the seed to the word of God.

Allegorization is a fun exercise and does demonstrate how parables can be used by the teaching church. Through the centuries, the Good Samaritan has also been frequently allegorized. You might want your students to do the following exercise. This parable especially teaches the theme of faith in action.

For your convenience in duplicating, the following material is reprinted on page 154 of the tear-out section in the teacher's manual.

Be a Good Samaritan (Please read Luke 10:29–37)

Jesus requires all of us to be Good Samaritans, to love even our enemies. This most popular of all parables has often been turned into an allegory through Christian history. Here is a popular interpretation of the parable.

Parable Elements	Allegorical Meaning	Your Interpretation
traveler	Adam (representing all humanity)	
Jerusalem	the heavenly city	
Jericho	the fallen world	
robbers	demons who strip Adam of immortality	
priest	Law	
Levite	prophets	
Samaritan	Jesus Christ (who heals humanity with oil and wine—comfort and admonition)	
inn	the church	
innkeeper	apostles: Peter and Paul	
Samaritan's return	second coming of Christ	

As a class, come up with your own allegory. Who are the victims of violence in *your* world? Who fails to take notice? What kind of aid can *you* and your classmates give? What would correspond to the inn?

Look at this parable in a creative way, interpret it in a modern-day setting, and then devise a service project where you and your classmates would actually give aid to a person who is hurting. Here are some examples: at an old folks' home; a hunger center; students in need of tutoring; etc. *Be a Good Samaritan!*

4. It would be appropriate at this time to develop a small service project for the group to perform. Allow them to suggest ways to serve. Tutoring grade-school children, buying a Disney videotape for a battered children's home, or a similar idea can help teach the students the importance of loving service.

Session 9: **Rejoice: The Reign of God Will Triumph**

1. Have the students read the section entitled "Rejoice." You might want to illustrate the parable of the yeast. Ask volunteers to bring flour, yeast, sugar and two pans to class. Then ask two other volunteers to make dough, knead it, put it in a pan and place it in a warm spot for the duration of the class. By the end of the class—if you are fortunate—the dough will have risen. Use this object lesson to illustrate the triumph of the reign of God. Students usually enjoy this "light touch."

2. Read through the parable of the "Sower and the Seed" as another metaphor for the triumph of the reign of God.

3. Present to the students that if God is the creator, then, by definition, there is nothing greater than God. Therefore, God will triumph because the creator is greater than creation. We have only to be on the winning team!

4. Use the theme of joy as an introduction to a penance service. This would be an excellent time to celebrate the Father's love and forgiveness. The themes of forgiveness and salvation make more sense when students are given the opportunity to experience our Lord's healing touch sacramentally. In planning the service, you might include the following elements:
   Readings: Use the parable of the Prodigal Son. As a commentary on the reading, students might dramatically read or enact any work they did on this parable or other parables of "the lost" in Luke 15.
   Music: The songs and the background music should emphasize love, forgiveness, salvation, or joy.
   Candles: Provide each student with a taper—lit from the paschal candle after the confession of sin—to indicate joy and the need to carry the message of love and divine forgiveness to others.
   Closing Prayer: Student-composed prayers of thanksgiving that acclaim God's love.

Session 10: **Summary and Evaluation**

1. Review the five summary statements with special attention to the seven points from Jesus' message. Clarify where needed.

2. Assign the following quiz:

For your convenience in duplicating, the following material is reprinted on page 155 of the tear-out section in the teacher's manual.

Quiz on Chapter 5

Name: _____

Date: _____

Part 1: Here is a summary of Jesus' message. Briefly explain what Jesus meant by each point.

1. Reign of God

2. Forgiveness

3. Abba

4. Salvation

5. Love and Judgment

6. Rejoice

Part 2: Select, read and briefly discuss the meaning of any three of Jesus' parables. Then explain how each parable teaches about God's reign.

Adaptation for Parish Religious Education Classes

Step 1: **Introduction** (15 minutes)

Begin by having the students work the opening exercise "Living Jesus' Teachings."

Step 2: **Teaching Style** (45 minutes)

1. Give each of the students an opportunity to teach something, anything, to the rest of the group. (You may need to allow some prep time the previous session.) We hope this will help them appreciate the creative teaching style of Jesus.

2. Have the students use the text to find eight facts about Jesus' teaching style. Write out their answers on the board. (See session 2 above.)

Step 3: **Jesus' Message** (30-minutes)

With enthusiasm and clarity, proclaim Jesus' message of the reign of God to the students. Use the parables featured in the chapter to supplement your presentation. Include a short witness talk telling the students how the Lord's message has touched your life. Invite the students to do the same.

chapter 6

Jesus

A Gospel Portrait

■ *introduction* ■

This chapter is straightforward and simple. It maintains that the gospels play an instrumental role in forming an accurate image of Jesus. Christian faith in Jesus must measure itself against the various gospel portraits of him.

The chapter introduces students to at least one dominant Christological theme in each of the four gospels. Thus, it presents a multi-faceted biblical view of Jesus. Jesus is the Servant Messiah in Mark, the New Moses in Matthew, the Savior of the World in Luke and the Word of God in John. A by-product of presenting these four major images of Jesus is to show students that, even at the time of the church's foundation, there was considerable Christological diversity. Each gospel evangelist was like an artist painting a portrait of Jesus, each seeing him in his own way, each being influenced by his community. Despite their diversity, each image is complementary and enormously insightful.

For this chapter to be most effective, we recommend that you assign all the scriptural passages suggested throughout the text. Also, if you have not yet assigned the complete reading of a gospel, this would be an ideal time in the course to do so.

Further Reading for the Teacher

Brown, S. S., Raymond E. *Biblical Reflections on Crises Facing the Church*. Mahwah, NJ: Paulist Press, 1975.

Please read Chapter 2, "'Who Do Men Say That I Am?'—A Survey of Modern Scholarship on Gospel Christology." This survey article situates the various biblical scholars who are doing Christology today. An outstanding contribution.

Brown, S. S., Raymond E. *The Community of the Beloved Disciple*. Mahwah, NJ: Paulist Press, 1979.

An outstanding work on the development of Johannine Christology.

Conzelmann, Hans. *The Theology of St. Luke*. Translated by G. Buswell. Philadelphia, PA: Fortress Press, 1982.

The book against which all studies of Luke-Acts must be measured. *The pioneering redactional criticism on Luke.*

Fitzmyer, S. J., Joseph A. *Christological Catechism: New Testament Answers*. Mahwah, NJ: Paulist Press, 1982.

An outstanding book, which you must read. It is short and timely. A great aid in teaching a course in Christology.

Freyne, Sean. *Galilee, Jesus, and the Gospels: Literary Approaches and Historical Investigations*. Philadelphia, PA: Fortress Press, 1988.

We recommend anything written by this outstanding scholar.

Kingsbury, J. D. *Jesus Christ in Matthew, Mark, and Luke*. Philadelphia, PA: Fortress Press, 1981.

A solid introduction to the Christology in each of the synoptics and Q. Looks at the titles used in each gospel, the ministry of Jesus, the passion narratives and the themes of community and discipleship.

Knopp, Robert. *Finding Jesus in the Gospels*. Notre Dame, IN: Ave Maria Press, 1989.

A wonderful, well-written introduction to the four gospels.

Marrow, Stanley B. *The Words of Jesus in Our Gospel: A Catholic Response to Fundamentalism*. Mahwah, NJ: Paulist, 1979.

A fine contribution. A good introduction to form and redaction criticism.

Senior, C. P., Donald. *Jesus: A Gospel Portrait*. Dayton, OH: Pflaum Press, 1975.

A popular book that does justice to its topic.

Shannon, William H. *Seeking the Face of God*. New York: Crossroad, 1988.

A wonderful book on Christian prayer and spirituality. Chapter 5 gives a great overview of the gospels and some major themes in Jesus' teaching. Excellent personal reading for teachers which also has some gems you can use with your students.

Stanley, S. J., David M. and Raymond Brown, S. S. "Aspects of New Testament Thought," *The Jerome Biblical Commentary*. No. 78. Englewood Cliffs, NJ: Prentice-Hall, 1969.

Important articles on topics such as the titles of Jesus, New Testament eschatology, kingdom of God, etc.

Suggested Audiovisual Ideas

Blessed Be . . . (8-minute color film, Paulist Productions). A film of a group of children with learning disabilities. The children recite the Beatitudes.

The Coming of Christ (28-minute color film, Films Incorporated). Traces Jesus' life up to the early public ministry. Artfully done.

Discovering the New Testament (60-minute, videocassette, Credence Cassettes). A scholarly introduction to the New Testament in eight presentations.

The Four Gospels (7½ hours, 4 videocassettes, Credence Cassettes). Four video presentations by Richard Rohr on the spirituality of the gospels.

The Gospel According to Luke (filmstrip with record, The Four Gospel Series, Alba House). A short overview of Luke's gospel.

The Gospel of Luke/The Gospel of Mark (13 units/4 parts, videocassette, ROA Media). Excellent commentary which can be used to supplement a couple of the sections of the student text.

He Is Risen for Us: According to Matthew/Mark/Luke/John (10/8/9/12.5-minutes, four films or videocassettes, Don Bosco Multimedia). Each short presentation provides an overview of the respective gospels.

Images of Christ (eight filmstrips, 9-10 minutes each, Thomas S. Klise). These "classics" can be used throughout the Jesus course.

Mark: Christian Kerygma (filmstrip with record or cassette, Service Evangelist Filmstrip Series, Paulist Press). Looks at Jesus' life in Mark's gospel. Produced by Father Terence J. Keegan, O.P.

The World of Jesus Christ: The Meaning of Christ's Life Today (42-minute color film, Mass Media Ministries). Examines Jesus' appeal to people in various cultures. Good on the theme of Jesus as the Savior of the world (Luke). Uses art images of the past 1000 years to develop the theme.

Whatsoever You Do (eight-minute color film, Films Incorporated). A documentary filmed on location in East Africa and in the United States. Makes the point that we respond to Jesus by responding to others.

Objectives

That students . . .

1. *Examine* how the gospels came to be.
2. *Identify* the three stages of gospel formation.
3. *Understand* the theory regarding the formation of the synoptic gospels.
4. *Distinguish* and *discuss* Jesus as the Servant Messiah, the New Moses, the Savior of the World and the Word of God as characterized by Mark, Matthew, Luke and John respectively.
5. *Explore* Jesus' understanding of the prophecies of the New Messiah and the Suffering Servant.

6. *Relate* certain prophecies from the Hebrew scriptures to Jesus concerning the coming of the Messiah.

7. *Appreciate* the universality and joy of Jesus' message as found in Luke.

8. *Reflect* on Jesus as the Word of God as found in John.

Time Used

Allow at least nine sessions to complete the material in this chapter. The gospels will be used extensively.

Procedure

Session 1: **Introduction**

1. Begin with Mark 16:15–16, the scripture quote that opens the chapter.

2. Write on the board the St. Jerome quote: "Ignorance of scripture is ignorance of Christ." Note the importance of the gospel as our fundamental source of knowledge about the historical Jesus. Define the three uses of the word *gospel*: the good news Jesus Christ proclaimed; Jesus himself; the written accounts of Jesus.

3. *Draw-a-picture exercise*:   Choose some interesting object for the students to draw. Perhaps select a student to serve as a model. Have the students sketch the model from their own vantage point. Do not allow them to move around the room. Allow them great latitude for creativity and fun. (This can also be done through a written description of what they see.) Share results. Draw the conclusion that each person sees reality from his or her own unique perspective. Yet, each person's drawing (or verbal portrait) offers new insight. Continue the analogy to the evangelists.

4. Work together the exercise entitled "Jesus, Good News and You."

5. For the next session, you might quiz students on the various meanings of the term *gospel*. Have them write the journal exercise for homework.

Session 2: **Gospel Formation**

1. You might begin with a demonstration to show how things take time to develop. For example, cut a golf ball in half and examine the various layers. Speculate on the process of how the golf ball was formed.

2. Explain that the gospels we have are finished products; they took time to develop. They went through a process.

3. Read through the material under the heading "Gospel Formation" and examine the three stages:

    1. *Historical Jesus* (6-4 B.C.–A.D. 30)

    2. *Early Church* (A.D. 30–65)—stories and sayings of Jesus preserved through oral tradition

    3. *Written gospels* (A.D. 65–100)
       Mark: 65–70

Matthew and Luke: 75–85
John: 90–100

4. After reviewing this material, allow students to construct their own gospel. Students can decide for themselves how they might do it. Of the following 15 sources, they can choose only 10. The first choice is the most important.

For your convenience in duplicating, the following material is reprinted on page 156 of the tear-out section in the teacher's manual.

The gospel according to _____.

Part 1: Examine the following sources and consider their importance for your gospel.

Sources:

A. Beatitudes (Sermon on the Mount)

B. Passion Narrative

C. Old Testament Prophecies

D. Healing Miracle Stories

E. Parables

F. Resurrection Accounts

G. Lord's Prayer

H. Reign of God Sayings

I. Proverbs

J. Infancy Narratives

K. Nature Miracle Stories

L. The Golden Rule

M. Jesus' Baptism and Temptation in the Desert

N. Jesus' Entry into Jerusalem

O. The Transfiguration

Part 2: Choose any 10 of the 15 sources that you consider are the most important. List them in your order of priority.

1: _____	6: _____
2: _____	7: _____
3: _____	8: _____
4: _____	9: _____
5: _____	10: _____

5. Allow students to defend their choices by having them compare them to those of the other students. Use this exercise as a way of understanding why

the gospel accounts of Jesus are different. Each evangelist was unique, with his own theology of Jesus, writing to a different audience. All these factors helped shape the formation of the gospels.

Session 3: **The Synoptics**

1. Ask students to bring in different portraits/pictures of Jesus. Ask them to identify what is different and similar about their pictures.

2. Read together the material on Stage 3 of the gospel formation. Diagram on the board the four-source theory of the synoptic gospels.

THE SYNOPTIC GOSPELS: A Theory on Their Composition

The Four-Source Theory:

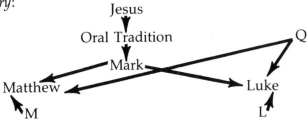

Q = short for *Quelle* (a German word meaning "source") used by both Matthew and Luke

M = material used only by Matthew

L = material known only to Luke

3. Explain that John developed from different sources (in particular, a discourse source). However, all four gospels have many facts in common.

4. To help your students apply the material they have learned, have them complete the following exercise below.

For your convenience in duplicating, the following material is reprinted on page 157 of the tear-out section in the teacher's manual.

Gospel Search

Place an X to indicate if a particular gospel takes up the theme or event listed.

	MT	MK	LK	JN	ALL	NONE
Birth of Jesus						
Slaughter of the Innocents						
Stable and Manger						
The Annunciation						
Baptism of Jesus by John						

	MT	MK	LK	JN	ALL	NONE
Temptation in the Desert						
Wedding Feast at Cana						
Beatitudes						
Parable of the Prodigal Son						
Peter's Commission						
Parable of the Good Samaritan						
Lord's Prayer						
Transfiguration						
Raising of Lazarus						
Jesus Enters Jerusalem						
The Last Supper						
The Passion						
Veronica Wipes Jesus' Face						
Jesus Falls Three Times						
Two Criminals Crucified						
Resurrection of Jesus						
Disciples on the Road to Emmaus						
Great Commission						
The Ascension						

Session 4: Mark's Jesus—The Servant Messiah

1. Introduce Mark's gospel as both the earliest and shortest. Then, begin discussing Mark's theme of Jesus as the Suffering Messiah. To follow Jesus, we must suffer as he did.

2. Review some of Mark's references to a human Jesus, discussed in the section entitled "A down-to-earth Jesus."

3. Review with the students the Isaiah prophecies regarding the Messiah and the Suffering Servant. Then read carefully Mark 8:27–33 where Jesus combines the two prophecies into one.

4. Research the Old Testament prophecies listed in the exercise, "Jesus the Messiah." Follow this with the discussion questions given or use ones of your own.

Session 5: Matthew's Jesus—The New Moses

1. Propose the following questions:

   a. Why is Matthew's gospel listed first in the New Testament?

b. Why would Matthew emphasize *prophetic fulfillment* throughout his gospel?

c. Why would the author of Matthew, writing to a Jewish-Christian audience, divide the teaching of Jesus into five sections?

d. What does Matthew propose to parallel the Ten Commandments?

2. Assure the students that an examination of this section will answer all these questions. Have them find the answers in the text.

3. As Moses taught the Ten Commandments, so Jesus now teaches us the new law. Work through the exercise on Matthew 18 as designated in the text. You might also ask students to check out the assignment on "Prophecies" given in the text.

Session 6: Luke's Jesus—The Savior of the World

1. Have students read the introductory paragraph of Luke and ask them: "Why could Luke's view of Jesus not be the same as Matthew's?" (Answer: Luke is writing to a Gentile-Christian audience. Gentiles would not relate well to images and prophecies derived from the Hebrew scriptures.)

2. Contrast Luke's picture of Jesus with Matthew's. Summarize Luke's portrait of Jesus by reading together the text's treatment of Luke's theme of joy and universal salvation. Pick out some favorite passages from Luke to read and discuss in class.

3. Assign the exercise entitled "Compassionate Touch." You might want to do the discussion exercise that follows.

4. A section of the film *Jesus of Nazareth* may be appropriate here. Choose some sections to illustrate the joyous Jesus.

Session 7: John's Jesus—The Word of God

1. Use a song like "On Eagle's Wings" from the *Glory and Praise* series for your opening prayer. Relate the symbol of the eagle to John's gospel.

2. Read through the material on John's gospel and present the major focus of Jesus as the Word of God. Choose some favorite passages from John to illustrate the "high Christology" presented there, for example, the Bread of Life or Living Water discourses.

3. Have students look through John and locate images of Jesus. The text lists some of them:

    Bread of Life

    Living Water

    Sheepgate

    Good Shepherd

    True Vine

    Light of the World

    Resurrection and the Life

    Word of God

4. Ask students to develop posters that promote following Jesus as the "way, truth and life."

5. Be sure to assign the exercise entitled "Faith in Jesus."

6. As a conclusion to this chapter, you might allow them time to write in their journals about their own unique theological image of Jesus.

Session 8: **Summary and Evaluation**

1. Be sure to read and reflect on the Prayer Reflection at the end of the chapter.

2. Review the summary statements and the focus questions. Clarify as needed.

3. Allow time to discuss any extended assignments you might have given, for example, reading a complete gospel.

4. The following can serve as a quiz for the chapter.

For your convenience in duplicating, the following material is reprinted on pages 158–159 of the tear-out section in the teacher's manual.

Quiz on Chapter Six

Name: _____

Date: _____

Part 1: *Match* each quotation below with one of the scriptural images of Jesus from Chapter 6 of the text.

> A — The Servant Messiah (Mark)
>
> B — The New Moses (Matthew)
>
> C — Savior of the World (Luke)
>
> D — The Word of God (John)

_____ 1. "My mother and my brothers are those who hear the word of God and put it into practice."

_____ 2. "I am the true vine, and my Father is the vinedresser."

_____ 3. "Then he looked angrily round at them, grieved to find them so obstinate. . . ."

_____ 4. "This was done to fulfill what the prophet had spoken."

_____ 5. "You are Peter, and upon this rock I will build my church."

_____ 6. "I tell you, there is rejoicing among the angels of God over one repentant sinner."

_____ 7. "He could work no miracle there because of their lack of faith."

_____ 8. "I am the good shepherd."

_____ 9. "Father forgive them; they do not know what they are doing. . . . This day, you will be with me in paradise."

_____ 10. Jesus went up to the mountainside and began to instruct them. "How blessed are the poor in spirit: the kingdom of Heaven is theirs."

Part 2:

List the three stages of gospel formation:

Stage 1: _____

Stage 2: _____

Stage 3: _____

Define the following terms:

kerygma: _____

synoptic: _____

Answers:

  1. C
  2. D
  3. A
  4. B
  5. B
  6. C
  7. A
  8. D
  9. C
10. B
Stage 1: historical Jesus (6/4 B.C.–A.D. 30)
Stage 2: oral preaching (A.D. 30–65)
Stage 3: written gospels (65–100)
kerygma: core teaching about Jesus
synoptic: "reading together"—Mark/Matthew/Luke

Adaptation for Parish Religious Education Classes

Step 1: **Introduction to the Gospels** (20 minutes)

1. Before the start of class, write out on the board the definitions of the term *gospel* along with a diagram of the three stages of gospel formation.

2. To explain briefly why the gospels give unique portraits of Jesus, choose some interesting object for the students to draw or describe. They must do so without moving around the room. Allow them latitude for creativity and fun. Share. Then, draw the conclusion that each person sees reality from his or her own perspective; each person's drawing/description offers new insight. Compare to the gospels.

3. Review the material on the board, explaining the process of how the gospels came to be formed.

Step 2: **Gospel Search** (30 minutes)

Use the exercise in *Session 3* entitled "Gospel Search" to show the differences among the various gospels. Have students work in groups of four or so.

Step 3: **The Four Gospels** (40 minutes)

1. Divide the class into four groups. Assign each group one of the four sections of the chapter that correspond to the four gospels.

2. Each group should prepare a short presentation on a particular image of Jesus expressed in its gospel.

3. Allow time for student presentations. List the various images discussed by the groups.

chapter 7

Jesus

A Personal Portrait

■ *introduction* ■

This chapter paints a portrait of Jesus, one that means something to today's students. It stresses certain inferences that can be drawn from a careful reading of the gospels. The task here is not to do "heavy theologizing" but to show that our Lord was a compelling human being who is the ideal of all we strive to be.

The chapter focuses on four qualities of Jesus: loving friend, sensitive and gentle, honest and courageous, and someone who respects women.

Our adolescents can imitate the specific qualities treated here. All of us need models and heroes, and Jesus is the perfect model of a human person. He manifested in his life an ability to show love and concern in a way that is attractive to today's youth. His gentleness, his friendship with people, his manner of teaching and his authenticity speak powerfully to those in search of self-identity. A discussion of how Jesus himself lived helps the personal growth and development of young Christians.

Finally, the chapter includes exercises that elicit student reflection on their own relationship with others and their personal integrity. Also, each session includes discussion questions to help generate thought and interest in this most fascinating person.

Further Reading for the Teacher

Bainton, Roland Herbert. *Behold the Christ*. New York: Harper & Row, 1974.

A generously illustrated book which depicts Jesus through the ages.

90

Bornkamm, Gunther. *Jesus of Nazareth*. San Francisco: Harper & Row, 1975.

This is a classic post-Bultmannian work on Jesus. Highly recommended.

Canale, Andrew. *Understanding the Human Jesus*. Introduction by Morton Kelsey. Mahwah, NJ: Paulist Press, 1985.

Written by a psychologist. Interesting reading which will help you construct your own "portrait" of the human Jesus.

Dodd, C. H. *Founder of Christianity*. New York: Macmillan, 1970.

This is an outstanding book, a favorite synthesis on Jesus. You must read it!

Endo, Shusaku. *A Life of Jesus*. Mahwah, NJ: Paulist Press, 1979.

A popular work on Jesus through the eyes of a non-Western author. A sensitive portrayal.

Green, Michael. *Was Jesus Who He Said He Was?* Ann Arbor, MI: Servant Publications, 1989.

In an entertaining and readable way, this book lines up the proof for Jesus and makes a case for his credibility for all the ages. A fun book to read.

Kaspar, Walter. *Jesus the Christ*. Translated by V. Green. Mahwah, NJ: Paulist Press, 1977.

One of the best of the Christologies developed in the 1970s. Orthodox and good.

Muggeridge, Malcolm. *Jesus: The Man Who Lives*. New York: Harper & Row, 1976.

The photography alone makes this book worth picking up. This personal portrait by the biographer of Mother Teresa is inspiring reading.

Nogosek, C. S. C., Robert J. *Nine Portraits of Jesus: Discovering Jesus Through the Enneagram*. Denville, NJ: Dimension Books, 1987.

You may or may not find the Enneagram a helpful road map to the spiritual life, but the reflections on Jesus are quite good.

Nouwen, Henri J. M. *Behold the Beauty of the Lord: Praying with Icons*. Notre Dame, IN: Ave Maria Press, 1987.

A beautiful book that teaches us how to pray with icons. We especially recommend Chapter 3 which has some warm insights on the Icon of the Savior of Zvenigorod.

Ouspensky, Leonid and Vladimir Lossky. *The Meaning of Icons*. Crestwood, NY: St. Vladimir's Seminary Press, 1982.

We really like icons and have used them in our own teaching, both to illustrate a method of prayer and a way of thinking about Jesus. This is a scholarly work on the topic with rich theology and abundant illustrations.

Sertillanges, A. D. *Jesus*. Denville, NJ: Dimension Books, 1976.

This reissued book by a leading French theologian/philosopher of the 1930s and 1940s applies the Ignatian insight of imagination in trying to picture the Jesus of the gospels. Traditional and very good.

Wahlberg, Rachel Conrad. *Jesus According to a Woman*. Mahwah, NJ: Paulist Press, 1975.

Somewhat of a landmark. Interesting and helpful.

Tapes:

Hellwig, Monika. *Who Is Jesus?* (NCR Cassettes). Kansas City, MO: National Catholic Reporter, 1976.

Suggested Audiovisual Ideas

Ecce Homo (28-minute, videocassette, Paulist Productions). The life, death, resurrection and ascension of Jesus are shown through great art masterpieces. Beautifully done.

The Face of Jesus (10-minute color film, Carousel Films). Narrated by Harry Reasoner, the film reverently tries to portray what Jesus might have looked like.

The Holy Shroud (filmstrip, Don Bosco). Tells the story of the alleged burial cloth of Jesus. You will, of course, want to supplement this with the latest research on the shroud. This enigmatic relic from the Middle Ages still fascinates scientists who have yet to figure out its origin.

The Grand Inquisitor (25-minute, 16mm film, Mass Media Ministries). From Dostoyevsky's great novel *The Brothers Karamazov*, pitting the prisoner, Christ, against authority. A great discussion starter. Useful for seeing the compassion and courage of Christ.

Images of Christ (eight color filmstrips, 9–10 minutes each, Thomas S. Klise). This set of filmstrips has been around for a while. They are all good and attempt to help the viewers formulate questions and shape their understanding of Jesus based on both "head" and "heart" knowledge of him.

Jesus of Nazareth (overhead transparencies and duplicating masters, Ikonographics). Gives an overview of Jesus' words and deeds.

Jesus of Nazareth (10 filmstrips or 684 slides, Don Bosco). The images are taken from the famous Zeffirelli film.

The Little Prince (27-minute, 16mm-animated, Mass Media Ministries). The essential nature of love is explored in this version of the Saint-Exupery classic.

Meet John Doe (134-minute, 16mm black & white film, Kit Parker Films). This Frank Capra classic serves as an allegory to Jesus and his ministry. The theme of friendship within a community is also developed.

Shua: The Human Jesus (60-minute, videocassette, Ave Maria Press). A dramatic performance on Jesus as seen through the life of a fictional friend. Good for drawing out the human Jesus.

Objectives

That students . . .

1. *Imagine* through prayerful reflection the physical appearance of the historical Jesus.

2. *Examine* some of the historical information about the physical nature of Jesus.

3. *Characterize* Jesus as a friend to all people.

4. *Respond* to Jesus' call to friendship.

5. *Cite* examples of Jesus' honesty and courage.

6. *Imitate* Jesus' personal integrity and commitment to all people.

7. *Recognize* the necessity of treating men and women equally, as modelled by Jesus.

8. *Develop* a positive picture of the human Jesus.

Time Used

Allow around eight class days to complete this material.

Procedure

Session 1: **Introduction**

1. For prayer, read the quote by Giles Fletcher that opens the chapter.

2. Select a student to read the opening story about the rabbi's lesson. Introduce the students to the chapter as an opportunity to look more closely at Jesus' human nature.

3. Present the following qualities of Jesus and discuss them. You might instruct students to memorize them for a quiz in a subsequent class. This list of eight is adapted from the book *On Being a Christian* by Hans Kung.

For your convenience in duplicating, the following material is reprinted on page 160 of the tear-out section in the teacher's manual.

Jesus the Person

What kind of person was Jesus? We can learn something of what a person is by what a person does, or doesn't do.

Jesus was . . .

1. **a lay person**: *not* a consecrated religious leader.

2. **a common person**: *not* a professional theologian or philosopher.

3. **a reformer**: *not* a revolutionary.

4. **someone who enjoyed life**: *not* an ascetic.

    (He ate and drank and accepted dinner invitations from the rich and poor alike.)

Jesus . . .

5. **preached the reign of God**: he was a teacher.

6. **lived God's will**: he went against some customs and laws, for example certain fasting and Sabbath regulations.

7. **spoke like a prophet**: he didn't worry about what people said or thought of him.

8. **identified himself with**:

> despised persons
> minorities
> heretics
> prostitutes
> adulterous people
> women
> political collaborators
> tax collectors
> lepers
> children

9. **lived his own words**: "Love your enemies."

> (Adapted from Hans Kung's *On Being A Christian*.)

4. Have the students work the exercise "The Human Jesus." Allow time to work on the journal exercise. Be sure to provide bibles.

5. If time remains, discuss their responses. This will give you a good feel for their knowledge of the human Jesus.

Session 2: **The Face of Jesus** (An optional unit.)

Our students always seem to enjoy a unit on what Jesus might have looked like. Here is some background material that you might wish to share with them.

For your convenience in duplicating, the following material is reprinted on pages 161–162 of the tear-out section in the teacher's manual.

The Face of Jesus

Jesus Christ is the most famous person who ever lived, yet we have no picture or painting of his real likeness. The Jewish religion of Jesus' day forbade personal portraits for fear of *idolatry*, the worshipping of false images. Nor do the gospels give us a physical description of Jesus. We simply don't know for certain if he was short or tall, plain-looking or handsome, dark or fair-skinned.

After several generations, Christians did begin to portray our Lord. The catacombs of Rome contain the earliest images of Jesus. There he appears as a curly-haired young man similar to young King David. At other times he appears as a bearded man with long hair, the style worn by pious Jewish men of Jesus' own day. Other early wall paintings show Jesus as the Good Shepherd, holding a lamb across his shoulders. Where Rome did tolerate Christian communities, Jesus appears as a teacher and a miracle-worker, his two main vocations described in the gospels. And after Constantine recognized Christianity, Jesus was increasingly shown as a heavenly king crowned in glory.

The early church Father, St. Jerome, concluded that some of God's majesty must have shown through Jesus' human body. He wrote:

> Had he not had something heavenly in his face and his eyes, the apostles never would have followed him at once, nor would those who came to arrest him have fallen to the ground (quoted in Denis Thomas, *The Face of Christ*, New York: Doubleday, 1979, p. 17).

Christian artists of later centuries largely adopted St. Jerome's view. Although a true representation of Jesus can never be captured, artists decided that paintings and statues of Jesus should be compatible with the beauty of the mystery of God becoming flesh. Jesus is *God*-made-man.

Only after about the year 1000 did paintings of Jesus as a suffering, crucified Savior become widespread. Depiction of a crucified Jesus appeared first in Byzantine art and then spread to the West. By the time of the Renaissance, artists increasingly portrayed a human Jesus. Rembrandt, for example, chose Jewish men from his city of Amsterdam as his models for Jesus. His paintings are excellent, classic representations. They portray a real man like us.

In the 19th century cheap, "syrupy" paintings of Jesus began to appear. Perhaps you have seen some of these. In them we see a delicate, "wimpy," soft-featured, almost effeminate Jesus. Missing is the strength that drove the money changers out of the Temple. Certainly, Jesus was no unassertive waxen image.

However we picture Jesus, we must consider three facts:

- He was a Jew who spent many hours on the road outdoors in the sun. He was surely tan, rugged, strong and chiseled by the elements. Traveling up and down the roads of Palestine took fierce drive and commitment.

- Jesus was a carpenter. He was a workingman with calloused hands. It takes strength and skill to hoist up cross beams, to cut timber and to work wood into useful implements.

- Jesus attracted all kinds of people. Strong, rough fishermen dropped their nets to follow him. The rich invited him to dinner. The poor, the sick and children longed for his touch. Women followed him around and cared for his needs. All types of people wanted to be his friend. There had to be something incredibly attractive about this Jesus of Nazareth.

1. Have the students read through the material in "The Face of Jesus." Be sure to bring in some art books and books on icons to illustrate the points in the essay.

2. Ask the students to describe how Jesus might have looked to his disciples.

3. Ask students to write a short description of how they picture Jesus.

4. This would be a perfect time to present a short film showing how Jesus has been depicted through the ages. (Check the A-V section above.) If you are unable to show a film, be sure to bring in a number of art books with representations of Jesus. They should span different periods of time and reflect different characterizations. If you have access to an opaque projector, use it to

project the pictures you have brought to class. Discuss the artists' conceptions. Ask the students to discuss why they like a particular representation better than another.

6. If you feel comfortable doing so, end this particular session with a silent meditation on Jesus. Seat the students in a circle. Darken the room. Ask for silence. Light a candle and place it in the middle of the circle. Put your favorite crucifix or artistic representation of Jesus next to the candle. Ask the students to meditate on Jesus.

Session 3: **Jesus as Friend**

Introduction:

We intend this section to be approached very positively! Many young people have problems with poor self-image and self-hatred. Merton Strommen's research still holds true: More than 20% of our students don't like themselves. Teenagers need to know that they are lovable, and unconditionally so. Our firm conviction is that Jesus dramatically reveals that we are lovable, so lovable that he calls us to be his friends, so worthwhile that he gave up his very life for us.

This section of the chapter is frankly evangelical. Our task as catechists is to share with our students the good news that Jesus and his Father love us and that they send to us the Spirit of love to dwell within. Our students need to know that Jesus calls them friends.

We have successfully taught these ideas through dramatic, faith-filled proclamation. You can use other techniques to communicate this central gospel idea, but we are convinced that enthusiastic witnessing is a most effective way.

1. Begin the session with a song, such as *Friends* by Michael W. Smith.

2. Have students list on the board as many friends of Jesus they can think of.

3. Assign a task whereby students show their appreciation for their best friend; for example, writing a letter, sending a gift, a verbal expression of love or the like. Another idea is to have the students make a new friend by corresponding with a prisoner. Ministry among inmates is sorely needed.

4. Together work the exercise "Friendship" and discuss how these qualities can be exhibited.

5. Perhaps some of your students would like to read and report on one of the following works on friendship and love. We have also used them successfully in teaching a theology of friendship.

James, Muriel and Louis Savary. *The Heart of Friendship*. New York: Harper & Row, 1978.

McGinnis, Alan Loy. *The Friendship Factor*. Minneapolis, MN: Augsburg Publishing House, 1979.

Powell, S.J. John. *The Secret of Staying in Love*. Valencia, CA: Tabor Publishing, 1974.

Powell, S.J. John. *Unconditional Love*. Valencia, CA: Tabor Publishing, 1978.

Ripple, Paula. *Called to Be Friends*. Notre Dame, IN: Ave Maria Press, 1980.

Session 4: **The Strong, Gentle Jesus**

1. For opening prayer, have someone read Mark 10:13–16. Discuss the following questions:

How does Jesus exhibit both strength and gentleness in this passage?

Are these two traits contradictory?

How can gentleness be strength?

How are these two traits paradoxical?

2. Have the students locate and list different groups that Jesus reached out to and made his friends.

Social Outcasts & Sinners—30 A.D.

lepers	children
women	Samaritans
tax collectors	Zealots
prostitutes	

Explain why these groups were considered outcasts and how Jesus responded to them. Develop another list of modern-day outcasts.

Social Outcasts & Sinners—1990s

homosexuals	punk rockers
communists	prostitutes
neo-Nazis	bikers
drug-users	drop-outs

Ask how Jesus might respond to these groups if he were here today in the flesh. (Emphasize that in a very real sense, *he is still here*, responding to them—through the Christians who call him Lord.)

3. Have the students search the scriptures to find further examples of how Jesus illustrated *strong* and *gentle* characteristics.

4. Use the exercise "Jesus: Strong, Yet Gentle" which lists additional references that students can research.

5. Carefully present the material in these pages. The stress on the nonverbal dimension might be a new thing for your students. It might prove helpful to have someone dramatically read the passages referred to above. Julius Fast's *Body Language* (Pocket Books, 1971) may help you demonstrate some of the nonverbal techniques which we use, most often unconsciously. The examples given in the text are merely a partial list of events that show Jesus' profound gentleness and concern for others. You may have the students make an additional list. Then, try to relate this to their lives by asking questions such as the following:

■ Is sensitivity a "manly" virtue? For example, what does it mean to be a *gentle*man? Do women define *gentleman* the same way men do?

■ Is sensitivity to others an admired virtue in today's society? in your school? Why or why not? How do television and the movies portray sensitivity in a person? Can a person be *macho* and sensitive at the same time? intelligent and sensitive? sexually attractive and sensitive?

- How is insensitivity shown in our school? at home? at work? at Mass? Can we do anything about it? What?

- Has anyone been particularly sensitive to you? When? How did the person show it, and how did it affect you?

- Does the laying on of hands at the conclusion of the rite of the sacrament of reconciliation mean anything to you in the context of this discussion? Explain.

Session 5: **The Honest, Courageous Jesus**

1. Read through the material in this section.

2. Young people are turned off by hypocrisy and phoniness. A good way to present Jesus is as a person who was the very opposite of all that is insincere and phony.

   Ask the students to define hypocrisy. Then discuss the following questions:

- Why don't you like a phony?

- Why do you admire integrity in a person?

- What are some risks of being genuine? (For example, a sincere person may be less popular because of his or her honesty.)

- Are a lot of people your age phony? Explain. (You may wish to discuss the problem of cheating here. Many teenagers do not like phonies, yet there is widespread cheating in schools. Why? Perhaps we admire honesty and integrity in others because we understand through our own failures how difficult it is to be consistently genuine.)

Cheating discussion questions:

- Cheating is a combination of what two sins?

- Is the pressure to cheat a justification or a rationalization?

- How many of you have cheated? (We are all sinners.)

- How do you cheat? Why do you cheat? What can be done about it? Should something be done?

- What is the courageous response to cheating?

3. Here is an exercise on personal honesty that you might want to use with your students:

For your convenience in duplicating, the following material is reprinted on page 163 of the tear-out section in the teacher's manual.

Honesty and You

Honesty is the touchstone of a person's character. It determines how genuine and authentic he or she really is. How do you measure up? How honest are you?

Answer the following questions as honestly as possible. Assume in all cases that you won't get caught.

98

	yes	no	?

1. Would you ever take a set of towels or an ashtray from a motel room in which you were staying? ____ ____ ____

2. If you found a wallet with $10 and the owner's identification, would you keep the money? ____ ____ ____

3. Would you ever lie about your work experience in filling out an application? ____ ____ ____

4. If your employer misfigured your hours and credited you with four hours you didn't work, would you not mention it and keep the money? ____ ____ ____

5. Would you make up a story to tell your parents rather than take your punishment for coming home late? ____ ____ ____

6. While pulling out of a tight spot in the shopping center, you dent the car parked next to you. You know it will cost a couple of hundred dollars to have it fixed. Furthermore, if you report the accident, your insurance rate will skyrocket. Would you leave without reporting the accident? ____ ____ ____

7. Would you cheat on a college entrance exam? ____ ____ ____

8. If a teacher praised you for your original, creative ideas on a topic when in fact you were just repeating what someone else had said in another class, would you let the teacher continue to think the ideas were your own? ____ ____ ____

Reflections: For a person of true integrity, "getting caught" is not an issue. Would you change any of your answers if the instructions above read: "Assume that what you do will become public knowledge." What does this say about your level of integrity?

4. Assign the journal exercises that conclude this section of the chapter.

Session 6: **Jesus and Women**

1. Assign the reading of this section and ask the students to cite:

- examples of how women in Jesus' time were the victims of discrimination
- examples of how Jesus upheld the dignity of women

2. As time permits, discuss some of the contemporary issues dealing with men and women. How might Jesus deal with these? Here are some examples:

- monogamy
- premarital sex
- male chauvinism
- abortion rights advocates
- surrogate motherhood

- gay/lesbian relationships
- pornography
- test-tube babies
- swimsuit editions of sports magazines
- music videos (and their portrayal of women)

Session 7: **Summary and Evaluation**

After you have reviewed the summary points and clarified any difficulties the students might be having, you might want to use the following quiz:

For your convenience in duplicating, the following material is reprinted on page 164 of the tear-out section in the teacher's manual.

Quiz on Chapter 7

Reflect on the following qualities of Jesus:

1. friendship
2. strength and gentleness
3. honesty and courage
4. treatment of women

In a well-written essay, give specific examples of how Jesus lived out these qualities. Use some of the insights from Chapter 7 to develop your argument. Make certain that your essay is coherent and organized. Perhaps developing a brief outline first may help.

Adaptation for Parish Religious Education Classes

Step 1: **Introduction—Friendship** (20 minutes)

1. Play the song "Friends" by Michael W. Smith as an opening prayer.
2. Introduce the concept of the human Jesus who invites you to friendship.
3. Have the students work the exercise "Friendship" on page **134**.

Step 2: **The Human Jesus** (60 minutes)

Show the students a film on the life of Jesus (such as an excerpt from Zeffirelli's *Jesus of Nazareth*). Have the students list the following qualities on a sheet of paper:

- anger
- strength
- compassion
- honesty
- sincerity
- courage
- equal treatment of women

Have the students observe examples of these traits in the film. Afterwards, discuss Jesus in relation to these qualities, using the material in this chapter as reference.

Step 3: **Prayer Service** (10 minutes)

Select a few volunteers to read aloud the Prayer Reflection that ends the chapter. You might want to discuss a bit what Jesus looked like. (See Session 2 above.) Be prepared with art books, holy cards, icons and the like.

chapter 8

The Paschal Mystery of Jesus

Passion, Death and Resurrection

▪ *introduction* ▪

This chapter takes up the paschal mystery, the saving events Jesus accomplished for us by virtue of his passion, death, resurrection and glorification.

The passion narrative is treated in some detail for several reasons. First, Jesus' suffering and death reveal God's great love for us. Students can grow to greater appreciation of the good news of our salvation by confronting the love Jesus poured out for us on the cross. Second, Jesus' last hours confirm the message he taught and the life he lived, topics treated earlier in the book. Jesus' passion and death are a living parable that reveals God's love at work in our midst. Third, prayerful reflection on Jesus' passion and death has drawn many Christians to the person of Jesus Christ himself. Helping our students draw closer to the living Lord must be the ultimate goal in a Christology course.

The second focus in the chapter is the resurrection of Jesus. This section stresses the absolute centrality of the *fact* of the resurrection and briefly discusses some of the biblical evidence that argues strongly that Christian faith is rooted in the ontological existence of Jesus as living Lord. We firmly reject the position that the resurrection is just a story meant to convey that Jesus' message lives on and other theories that deny the reality of the resurrection.

The last section of the chapter challenges students to reflect on the meaning of the paschal mystery for their personal lives. The true meaning of life is found in imitation of Jesus' death and resurrection. We are all called to die to self, to sacrifice, to love. By dying to self and reaching out to others in imitation of the Lord, we will experience true living.

Further Reading for the Teacher

Brown, S. S., Raymond E. *The Virginal Conception and Bodily Resurrection of Jesus*. Mahwah, NJ: Paulist Press, 1973.

> An excellent work which carefully analyzes the data of the resurrection narratives. His scholarly conclusions are balanced and orthodox. Must reading.

Durrell, F. X. *The Resurrection: A Biblical Study*. New York: Sheed and Ward, 1960.

> This seminal work in Catholic scholarship did much to recapture the central role the resurrection plays in salvation history.

Fuller, R. H. *The Formation of the Resurrection Narratives*. Philadelphia, PA: Fortress Press, 1980.

> An insightful work on the resurrection narratives. Comprehensive and clearly written.

Lohfink, Gerhard. *The Last Days of Jesus*. Notre Dame, IN: Ave Maria Press, 1984.

> A thoroughly engrossing reflection on the passion. Presents the crucifixion in the historical and cultural context of Jewish and Roman intrigues.

Moltmann, J. *The Crucified God*. San Francisco: Harper & Row, 1974.

> Reminds us of the proper role of Jesus' crucifixion.

O'Collins, Gerald. *Interpreting the Resurrection*. Mahwah, NJ: Paulist Press, 1988.

> Father O'Collins is one of our very favorite scholars. This is an excellent defense of the traditional belief in the resurrection. We recommend everything he writes.

Perkins, Pheme. *Resurrection: New Testament Witness and Contemporary Reflection*. New York: Doubleday, 1984.

> A readable treatment of the topic.

Perrin, Norman. *The Resurrection According to Matthew, Mark, and Luke*. Philadelphia, PA: Fortress Press, 1977.

> An excellent summary of the resurrection narratives.

Suggested Audiovisual Ideas

Attention Must Be Paid (28-minute color film, Paulist Productions). An allegory of a dying man (Jesus-figure) who ministers to others and shows them unconditional love, even in the midst of his own sufferings.

Bible News—Jesus Programs series, "The Arrest," "The Trial," "Crucifixion and Resurrection" (records or cassettes, Twenty-Third Publications). These three presentations use a radio format to depict the events.

Christ In His Own Land (23 & 24-minute segments, Parts 9 & 20, filmstrip and cassette, Don Bosco Multimedia). This documentary examines the land highlighted from Palm Sunday to the Crucifixion.

Greater Love (13-minute color film, Mass Media Ministries). Based on the true story of a child who was willing to offer her rare blood to save her brother's life. An example of simple love and sacrifice that is a modern-day parable of Jesus' love for us.

He Is Risen (29-minute color film, Films Incorporated). A sequel to *The Coming of Christ*. Portrays the late public ministry of Jesus.

He Is Risen for Us: A Biblical Study on the Resurrection According to Matthew, Mark, Luke and John (four color filmstrips with cassettes and study guides, Don Bosco Films). Presents the resurrection from the viewpoint of each of the evangelists.

"The Son of God Crucified" and "The Risen Lord Lives Forever," *Jesus of Nazareth* (21 & 24-minute color film segments, Parts 13 & 14, Don Bosco Multimedia). The segments of the classic Zeffirelli film present the passion and resurrection of Jesus.

Jesus the Redeemer (45-minute, videocassette, Teleketics). A guided tour of the parts of the Holy Land involved in the passion, death and resurrection of Jesus.

The Last Days of Jesus (70-frame filmstrip with cassette and study guide, Alba House). Relives the steps of Jesus from Olivet to Calvary.

One Who Was There (37-minute color film, Mass Media Ministries). Depicts a woman who is the first to experience the risen Lord and her gradual understanding that she must continue life's journey in the spirit of the resurrection: to serve the living, especially those who need her.

Parable (22-minute color film, Mass Media Ministries). A classic allegory that evokes Jesus' passion in the story of a ministering clown in a traveling circus.

Resurrection (27-minute color film, Paulist Productions). An allegorical film that depicts Jesus struggling against temptation that challenges his true identity. Ends with Jesus rejoining his brothers and sisters on earth to give their lives freedom and meaning.

Suffering to Glory (two-cassette program, NCR Cassettes). Scripture scholar Father Eugene LaVerdiere examines the passion and resurrection narratives.

The Velveteen Rabbit (15-minute, 16mm color film, Mass Media Ministries). A parable of resurrection emphasizing the centrality of love.

Objectives

That students . . .

1. *Read* and prayerfully *reflect* on the passion narratives of Jesus.

2. *Know* the major events of Jesus' last days.
3. *Discuss* the meaning of Jesus' passion, death, resurrection and glorification in salvation history.
4. *Memorize* and *interpret* Jesus' last words.
5. *Critique* some of the false notions of Jesus' resurrection.
6. *Reflect* on the meaning of the paschal mystery for their own faith lives.
7. *Appreciate* what it means to be people of the cross and resurrection people.

Time Used

Allow around nine class days to develop and discuss the material in this chapter.

Procedure

Session 1: **Introduction**

1. Use the prayer of St. Patrick on the opening page to introduce the chapter.
2. Read together the introductory material on the significance of the cross as a sign of Christ's love for us.
3. To stress the symbolism of the cross, bring various crucifixes to class. Ask the students for their *emotional* reactions when they see a crucifix. You might also bring books on Christian symbols. Some students may wish to decorate the room with symbols of Jesus.
4. As a pre-test of student knowledge about Jesus' passion, you could use the quiz provided in the text. The journal suggestions at the end of the quiz can help to review the basic content of the passion narrative.
5. Set up a calendar of key readings for the students to do for homework throughout the chapter. Each section of material contains scripture references.

Session 2: **The Last Supper**

1. Review together the information under the sections "Palm Sunday" and "Holy Thursday."
2. Afterwards, have the students identify any parallels between the Jewish Passover and the Last Supper. Here are some parallels you may want to highlight:

JEWISH PASSOVER	JESUS' LAST SUPPER
1. a table *meal of fellowship*	1. a final table *meal of fellowship*
2. the *words* of the exodus account of the first Passover are spoken	2. the bread and wine were blessed and distributed with the *words*: "This is my body." "This is my blood." "Do this in memory of me."
3. by remembering God's saving presence at the time of the Exodus, *God once again becomes present*	3. by re-enacting this event, *Christ becomes present* in us through the mystery of the Mass
4. the *Paschal Lamb* is a symbol of Jewish social salvation	4. Christ is our *Paschal Lamb* —a symbolic title of our personal salvation

3. *Optional*: Invite a priest to your classroom and organize and celebrate a Mass together. Try to involve as many students as you can and make the celebration as intimate as possible. Our students are hungering for a real experience of Eucharist. This is an opportunity to provide it.

Session 3: **The Passion**

1. Use one of the following three approaches:

Approach 1: If you chose to have the students read the John, Mark and Luke sections in class, read together the passion narrative of Matthew. As you go through Matthew:

   a. Have the students compare and contrast Matthew's narrative with accounts they read in class (Mark, Luke or John).

   b. Pause periodically to draw out the significant points discussed on pages 147–152 of the text.

Approach 2: Show one of the audiovisuals annotated above. In your discussion of the work, have the students add details from their reading of the passion narratives.

In either Approach 1 or Approach 2, highlight these points:

■ the significance of the Last Super celebrated in the context of a Passover meal (see Session 2)

■ the desire of the man Jesus to avoid a painful death

■ the charges against Jesus and the Roman role in his crucifixion

■ the significance of the seven last words of Jesus (Incidentally, we strongly recommend that you require your students to memorize these. See the concluding Prayer Reflection.)

Approach 3: If you did not use this exercise earlier, have the students create a newspaper account of the Holy Week events based on Matthew's version. When the project is finished, discuss the following: What kind of literary forms make up your newspaper? How are these like or unlike the gospel as literary form?

Here is a suggested format for the newspaper:

For your convenience in duplicating, the following material is reprinted on page 165 of the tear-out section in the teacher's manual.

Dateline Jerusalem

Imagine that you and your classmates are staff members of the *Jerusalem Gazette*. You are to produce a Saturday morning edition reporting the crucifixion of Jesus and the events leading up to it.

Sample Story Ideas:

1. *Obituary* for Jesus of Nazareth
2. *News stories* summarizing the events of Holy Week
3. *In-depth interviews*:

■ *with Jewish and Roman officials*: members of the Sanhedrin, Pontius Pilate, Pilate's wife, Herod, the Roman centurion at the site of the crucifixion, etc.

■ *with Jesus' friends*: Mary, Peter, John, Joseph of Arimathea, Lazarus and the like

■ *with Judas* (you might also report his death)

■ *with Jesus' mother*

4. *Background features*: the Roman law of occupation and capital punishment, the workings of the Sanhedrin, the method of crucifixion, burial practices in Palestine
5. *Weather report*
6. *Editorials*: one supporting Jesus' condemnation and one opposing it
7. *Letters to the Editor*: from the mother of the "good" thief, Barabbas, Simon of Cyrene and others
8. *An account of the Last Supper* given by an apostle, perhaps Thomas

Let your imagination suggest other story ideas. Perhaps some students could do line drawings of the arrest, trial and crucifixion. Others could devise ads and be responsible for the layout and design of the paper.

2. Have the students work the exercise "Courage" on pages 152–153. Use the "Discuss" questions in light of the passion.
3. If time permits, allow students to begin the journal exercise that follows in the text.

Session 4: **The Crucifixion**

1. Show a segment of a film that portrays the crucifixion (Zeffirelli's film is annotated above).
2. Read carefully the material in the section "The Crucifixion" on the interesting physical details of the crucifixion. Discussing the information can give the students an appreciation of what Jesus experienced.
3. Explain the term *Via Dolorosa* and then play the song "Via Dolorosa" by Sandy Patti.
4. Have a contest to see who can find and write down the last words of Jesus (a total of seven statements from the four gospels) first.
5. Use the Prayer Reflection at the end of the chapter as a prayerful meditation on the last words of Jesus.

Session 5: **Resurrection of Jesus**

1. Have the students read the empty tomb accounts in the Synoptics:

    Mk 16:1–8   Mt 28:1–8   Lk 24:1–12

Ask the following questions:

a. What *differences* do you see in the details of the three accounts? (Underline any differences noted in the text.)

b. What *similar elements* are in all three accounts?

c. What is the common reaction given by the women (and disciples) to the witness of the empty tomb?

2. The resurrection is fundamental to our faith. We assert the factual reality of Jesus' resurrection. The section "What happened?" affirms this truth against the modern denials of non-believers. Allow an opportunity for questions.

3. Outline the five notions of the afterlife. Explain why the other notions are false.

4. Some films annotated above illustrate the resurrection. Perhaps a short film here can help in presenting this material.

5. Studying the death and resurrection of Jesus provides a good opportunity to contemplate our own attitudes toward death. If you want to touch on this topic, do the following exercises with your students. The research project could be used as a homework assignment.

For your convenience in duplicating, the following material is reprinted on page 166 of the tear-out section in the teacher's manual.

Attitude Toward Death

Christian belief in a personal resurrection through Jesus Christ should affect your attitude toward death. React to the following statements.

5 — strongly agree
4 — agree
3 — don't know
2 — disagree
1 — strongly disagree

_____ 1. I'd like at least 24 hours to prepare for my death.

_____ 2. I'd like to know how I am going to die.

_____ 3. It is foolish to worry about death.

_____ 4. It is wrong to fear death.

_____ 5. I feel uneasy around dying people.

_____ 6. Death leads to resurrection.

_____ 7. How I live will make a difference when I die and meet my judgment.

_____ 8. Those who believe in Jesus will be raised on the last day.

Share and discuss your responses.

Heaven. Complete these open-ended sentences.

1. When I see the Lord in the afterlife, I will thank him for . . .
2. When I see the Lord in the afterlife, I will ask him . . .
3. A famous person I would like to see in heaven is . . .
4. The person I want to spend eternity with is . . .
5. Heaven will be like . . .
6. Belief in my personal resurrection . . .

Optional: Share your responses and discuss the attitudes that they reveal.

Research: Choose one of the following religions or cults and research its beliefs about the afterlife:

- Aztec or Incan religion
- Hinduism, Buddhism, or Islam
- Judaism
- Christianity
- a modern cult
- ancient Roman or Greek religion

  Report your findings to the class.

Session 6: **Resurrection Appearances**

1. Begin by allowing students to work the journal exercise on page 157 which deals with the resurrection appearances. They might wish to work in groups of two or three.

2. After examining the appearance accounts, ask students to identify how the disciples understood the nature of the resurrected Christ. It seems that the disciples themselves did not understand the nature of the risen Christ.
   You can place some of the observations in two categories:

Things only a glorified body could do	Things only a physically present human being can do
Jesus was alive after his death, suddenly appearing in the room, even though the door was locked.	Jesus talked to his disciples, telling them, "Peace be with you."
Jesus changed his appearance at will so that he was not recognized until he desired to be known.	Jesus ate food. He even cooked some food and served it. He asked Thomas to touch his wounds.
He left the room as he had entered, simply vanishing from sight.	He left them consoled and assured them the person they were seeing and talking to was the very same Jesus they had known for three years.

We can learn from the "Appearance Accounts" that:

- Jesus was really *risen*, and really *alive!*
- Jesus did not come back to *this* life at all.

- The early church did *not* fully *understand* the nature of Jesus.
- Jesus had a new and totally unique *resurrected* existence.

3. Discuss the various ways that Christ still makes his presence known. Recall that Christ is present when you do something for the least of your brothers and sisters. Responding to them is responding to the Lord. Elicit examples of supernatural occurrences where people claim to see a visible Christ. Emphasize that Christ is more present in our fellow human beings than in an image of Christ reported.

Session 7: **Paschal Mystery**

1. Define *paschal mystery* for the students using the "Living Jesus' Passion, Death and Resurrection" section of the chapter.

2. Review some of the ways that the students can live out the paschal mystery. Draw from insights discussed in the section "Imitating Jesus." List the points on the board or overhead.

3. The students should work and discuss the exercise "Witnessing to the Lord."

4. To give a historical perspective on the paschal mystery, show how the concept is universal. For example: A tree must give up its fruit (die to self) in order to grow and bear fruit in spring (rise to self). Research and present to the students the stories of:

- the Phoenix bird (Egyptian)
- the death of King Arthur (English)
- the death of Hercules (Greek)

These stories are from different cultures and different times, but they all share a common desire for life after death. Yearning for an eternal existence is basic to human nature. Jesus' historical passion, death and resurrection fulfills the universal hope of humanity.

You may want to review an example of this through a musical presentation. The song from the rock group *Yes* presents a song entitled "Turn of the Century" on the album entitled *Going for the One*. It is based on a Nordic myth about a sculptor who sculpts the image of his deceased wife, and in the end, the image comes to life. His wife Roan is reborn.

5. If time permits, discuss student beliefs about the afterlife. Proclaim the Christian teaching on this subject. Using the exercise below, you may want them to interview people, or just respond to the statements themselves.

For your convenience in duplicating, the following material is reprinted on page 167 of the tear-out section in the teacher's manual.

Heaven and Hell

Answer these questions in complete paragraphs. Do you agree or disagree with the following positions? Why or why not?

1. Heaven is an eternal state but we don't know what it is physically like.

2. There is a hell and people are in it.

3. Life will continue forever after death for those who live like Jesus commanded.

4. Hell is annihilation—the total discontinuation of life and existence.

5. Heaven is a possibility for everyone.

6. Heaven and Hell begin here, and continue in the afterlife.

7. Not everyone will receive eternal life, because God determined all before you were born.

Session 8: **Evaluation**

1. Review the major points of the chapter. For their quiz, ask them to write 25–50 factual statements about the passion and resurrection narratives. Give them one point for each statement that is correct.

2. Be sure to assign the first exercise in the journal entries at the end of the chapter.

Adaptation for Parish Religious Education Classes

Step 1: **Introduction** (5 minutes)

For the opening prayer, play a song that relates to Jesus' passion.

"Via Dolorosa" by Sandi Patti

"The Crucifixion" from *Godspell*

"The Crucifixion" from *Jesus Christ Superstar*

Step 2: **The Passion and Crucifixion** (45 minutes)

1. Show a segment of a film that portrays the crucifixion. (Zeffirelli's film is annotated above.)

2. Read carefully the material in the section "The Crucifixion" on the interesting physical details of the crucifixion. Discussing the information can give the students an appreciation of what Jesus experienced.

3. Have the students find the seven last statements of Jesus during his passion. Briefly comment on the significance of each.

Step 3: **The Resurrection** (40 minutes)

1. Together read one of the resurrection appearance accounts. (They are listed in the chapter.)

2. The resurrection is fundamental to our faith. We assert the factual reality of Jesus' resurrection against modern denials. We suggest that you proclaim the message of the resurrection to the students and supplement this with witnessing why it is true.

3. Some films annotated above illustrate the resurrection. Perhaps a short film here (if not used in Step 1) can help in presenting this material.

4. For further discussion, the "Attitude Toward Death" exercise listed in Session 5 of this book can be helpful.

5. If time remains, mention our need to live the paschal mystery in our own lives. Assign and discuss the "Witnessing to the Lord" exercise at the end of the chapter.

chapter 9

Belief Through the Ages

■ *introduction* ■

This chapter surveys the church's traditional beliefs about Jesus, especially ones hammered out in the early councils. It is probably the most cognitively difficult chapter in the text, but for us to neglect the tradition of the church would be a great disservice to our students. We believe that Jesus lives in the church, his body, and that he continues to teach through it. The church's tradition is a wonderful source of light on the person of Jesus.

After introducing Jesus as a person of fundamental importance in human history, the chapter begins by examining key symbols and titles of Jesus. Titles such as Lord, Son of God, Prophet, High Priest and King present an orthodox understanding of the nature of Jesus. The exercise "False Images" shows the contemporary heterodox images of Jesus that are widespread.

After some preliminary remarks on the church's need to clarify doctrine on Jesus, the chapter takes up the history of the early councils and their teaching in the area of Christology. Doctrinal development typically took place in reaction to false beliefs and teachings about Jesus. The chapter discusses why these heresies were (and are) dangerous and show the biblical basis for the philosophical definitions of Jesus that emerged from the councils.

We then turn to the Nicene Creed as our fundamental profession of faith, giving theological comments in a line-by-line analysis of this classic statement of faith.

The chapter concludes by examining two popular questions concerning Jesus. The questions "Did Jesus have brothers and sisters?" and "Who is respon-

112

sible for Jesus' death?" are addressed in light of church teaching. The students are given an opportunity to examine their own prejudice toward the Jews in the exercise "Love Your Enemy."

Further Reading for the Teacher

Bokenkotter, Thomas. *Essential Catholicism: Dynamics of Faith and Belief*. New York: Doubleday, 1986.

Chapters 5–7 give a fair appraisal of the current Christology being done today.

Borowitz, Eugene B. *Contemporary Christologies: A Jewish Response*. Mahwah, NJ: Paulist Press, 1980.

A critical examination of theological views of Jesus from a Jewish perspective. Written by a highly regarded spokesman.

Brown, Raymond E. *Jesus, God and Man*. New York: Macmillan, 1967.

See especially the outstanding essay entitled "How Much Did Jesus Know?"

Chesnut, Glenn F. *Images of Christ: An Introduction to Christology*. San Francisco: Harper and Row, 1984.

Treats different images of Jesus in its approach to Christology. The chapter on Christ's humanity gives an interesting overview of the question.

Cook, Michael L. *The Historical Jesus*. Chicago: Thomas More Press, 1986.

An easy-to-read portrait of Jesus.

Helminiak, Daniel A. *The Same Jesus: A Contemporary Christology*. Chicago: Loyola University Press, 1986.

Kelly, J. N. D. *Early Christian Doctrines*, rev. ed. San Francisco: Harper & Row, 1978.

A classic source book.

Lawler, Ronald, Donald W. Wuerl, and Thomas Comerford Lawler. *The Teaching of Christ*, 2nd ed. Huntington, IN: Our Sunday Visitor Press, 1983.

The bibliography supplies a handy cross-reference for the councils and their theological formulations.

Marthaler, O.F.M.Conv., Berard L. *The Creed*. Mystic, CT: Twenty-Third Publications, 1986.

An outstanding work. The best of its kind. Highly recommended. This will enrich your teaching of this chapter.

McBrien, Richard. *Catholicism*. San Francisco: Harper and Row, 1980.

Chapter 11 through 16 brilliantly synthesize the whole of Christology. This is an excellent work to refer to as you teach a course in Christology.

Moran, Gabriel. *The Present Revelation*. New York: Herder and Herder, 1972.

Moran's chapter on the Jewish and Christian experience of revelation is one of his best.

Pannenberg, W. *Jesus: God and Man*. Translated by L. Wilkins and D. Priebe. Louisville, KY: Westminster/John Knox Press, 1982.

> An outstanding respected history of Christology from New Testament times through the present.

Pelikan, Jaroslav. *Jesus through the Centuries*. San Francisco: Harper and Row, 1987.

> The best cultural history of Jesus we've seen. A survey of Christology, especially how it incarnates itself in the art and life of the people. Highly recommended.

Rahner, Karl. "Dogmatic Reflections on the Knowledge and Self-Consciousness of Christ, " *Theological Investigations*, Vol. 5. New York: Crossroad, 1966.

> A sophisticated study that has influenced most subsequent writing on the topic. Worth wading through.

Sloyan, Gerard S. *The Jesus Tradition: Images of Jesus in the West*. Foreword by Donald Senior, C. P. Mystic, CT: Twenty-Third Publications, 1986.

> A gem that gives the reader many images of Jesus down through the centuries, especially through the eyes of saints and writers of classic spiritual works. Illuminating work.

Timmerman, John. *A Layman Looks at the Names of Jesus*. Wheaton, IL: Tyndale House Publishers, Inc., 1985.

> This book will give you a wealth of ideas for teaching the titles of Jesus with good scriptural and prayer reflections added for each title treated.

Suggested Audiovisual Ideas

The Council of Nicea (filmstrip, United Church Press). Covers the background, proceedings and results of the council.

Godspell (103-minute, 16mm, Clem Williams Films Inc.). The dated musical based on the words of Matthew—a good discussion starter for contemporary views on Jesus.

The Happy Prince (25-minute color film, videocassette, Mass Media Ministries). Oscar Wilde's classic story of redemptive love offers yet another title for Jesus.

Hunger for Jesus, The Bread of Life (16-minute color filmstrip with cassette, "The Eucharist" series, Don Bosco Multimedia). A good reflection of this powerful title of Jesus—relating both to physical and spiritual hunger.

"Jesus Lives in His People," *Acts of the Apostles* (26-minutes, Part 2, 16mm, Don Bosco Multimedia). This segment tells the story of the early church's beginning struggles.

Jesus B.C. (27-minute, videocassette, Insight: Paulist). A story about the necessity of the Incarnation from the point of view of the Trinity.

Little Falls Incident (7-minute color film, Anti-Defamation League of B'nai B'rith). An excellent film about prejudice in American society. Details an anti-Semitic incident in a junior high school. Includes a helpful teacher's guide with role-playing ideas and suggestions on how to deal with stereotyping and prejudice. Good for a community which is convinced that anti-Semitism is not a problem.

Night and Fog (31-minute black and white film, McGraw-Hill). An explicit documentary of the atrocities committed during the Holocaust. An unforgettable classic.

Thunder in Munich (27.5-minute, black and white Insight Film, Paulist Productions). An excellent drama about the witness of Father Meier, a priest who warned his people that no one can be a good Catholic and a Nazi at the same time. An excellent film on universal brotherhood and resistance to tyranny.

Objectives

That students . . .

1. *Appreciate* the value of symbols and titles that express faith in Jesus.
2. *Critique* some false images of Jesus in contemporary culture.
3. *Identify* certain heresies that developed about Jesus and *discuss* why they were a threat to Christianity.
4. *Know* and *discuss* the classic dogmatic formulations about Jesus taught at the early councils and reaffirmed today.
5. *Memorize* and *explain* the Nicene Creed.
6. *Discuss* certain modern issues of Christology including the question of the brothers and sisters of Jesus and the problem of anti-Semitism.
7. *Examine* their own prejudices.

Time Used

Allow eight classes for this material. Additional time may be needed for an in-depth explanation of the heresies.

Procedure

Session 1: **Introduction**

1. As an opening prayer, listen to "Emmanuel" by Amy Grant. The song uses Isaiah's messianic titles.
2. Read the introductory section of the chapter. Have the students respond to the question, "How has the world changed because of Jesus?" Be sure to give your own answer to this question. Include how both the physical world and the spiritual world have changed.
3. To introduce the power and value of symbols, ask the students to identify the significance of the following symbols:
   a. green jacket (Master's Golf Tournament)
   b. Lombardi trophy
   c. Wimbleton Cup

      d. Olympic Gold Medal

      e. Black belt (in karate)

      f. crucifix

      g. statues

      h. holy water

      i. incense

      j. St. Francis medal

4. Explain that human beings are symbol makers and that symbols are not just a "Catholic oddity." Then, have them work the exercise entitled "Faith in Symbol." Be sure to share.

Session 2: **Titles of Jesus**

1. Read or refer to the opening remarks of this section of the chapter.

2. Titles are used to describe individuals only if they have done something worth remembering. Most individuals would consider themselves fortunate if they were known by just *one* symbol. Yet Jesus is know by many. To appreciate the use of titles, you might have the students identify the following.

Easy

President of the U.S.A.	current president
Pope	current pope
The Lone Eagle	Charles Lindbergh
King of Late Night TV	Johnny Carson
Iron Mike	Mike Tyson
The Greatest	Muhammad Ali
The King of Rock and Roll	Elvis Presley
The Duke	John Wayne
Magic	Erwin Johnson
The Boss	Bruce Springsteen
The Father of America	George Washington
The Emancipator	Abraham Lincoln

Harder

The Golden Bear	Jack Nicklaus
The Say-hey Kid	Willie Mays
The Bronx Bomber	Babe Ruth
Sweetness	Walter Payton
The Buddha	Siddartha Gautama
The Desert Fox	General Erwin Rommel
The Great One	Jackie Gleason

The Galloping Ghost	Red Grange
The Yankee Clipper	Joe DiMaggio

Scripture
(not including Jesus)

The Baptist	John the Baptist
The Lawgiver	Moses
The Mother of God	Mary

Have students add any titles they can. Add your own favorites to this list and let it expand each year.

3. Pose the question: "Why do we use titles?" Elicit the answer: "They describe in a nutshell an understanding of a person. They shed light on how and what we believe about someone."

4. Review the titles Lord, Son of God, Prophet, High Priest and King as treated in the student text. Describe what they say about the person of Jesus. Remind students that in an earlier chapter they read about Jesus as Messiah, Son of Man, Suffering Servant, Word of God and others.

5. The following is designed to give students an appreciation of the vast number of titles of Jesus. These indicate the power he has over the human imagination and his significance for human history.

   A. Pass out old missalettes to students and challenge them to page through them to find as many titles of Jesus as possible.

   B. *Title Search*:   Have students identify the following titles of Jesus found in scripture. Answers are provided for your convenience, according to the *New Jerusalem Bible*.

Hebrew Scriptures	(Answers)
Is 9:6	Prince of Peace, Mighty God, Wonder-Counselor
Mal 3:20	Sun of Justice
Jer 31:31	New Covenant
New Testament	
Jn 10:11	Good Shepherd
Jn 4:14	Living Water
Jn 6:35	Bread of Life
Jn 1:4,5,9	Light of the World
Mt 9:12–13	Divine Physician
Acts 17:31	Judge
Mk 1:24	Holy One
Jn 1:29	Lamb of God
Acts 3:15	Prince of Life
Rev 15:3	Lord God Almighty
Rev 5:5	Lion of the Tribe of Judah

Rev 22:16	Root of David
Rev 22:16	Morning Star
Rev 19:16	King of Kings
Rev 1:8	Alpha and Omega
1 Jn 1:1	Word of Life
1 Jn 2:1	Advocate
Jn 14:6	Way, Truth, Life
Lk 1:78	Rising Sun
Lk 1:69	Saving Power
Acts 10:36	Lord of All
Jn 8:58	I Am
Jn 1:34	Chosen One of God
Jn 11:25	Resurrection
Jn 1:41	Messiah
2 Pt 2:20	Savior
Eph 2:20	Cornerstone
1 Pt 2:25	Shepherd and Guardian of Souls
2 Tm 4:8	Upright Judge
Eph 1:22	Head of the Church
Acts 15:11	Lord Jesus
1 Pt 5:4	Chief Shepherd
Mt 2:6	Leader
Acts 3:13,25	Servant

Session 3: **False Images**

1. Discuss the power of titles. Is there any danger to using titles? Can a title mislead? Are there infamous titles as well as famous ones?

2. Work the following exercise which reviews three contemporary images of Jesus. Have the students use scripture to find passages to refute these titles. Be sure to evaluate what students come up with for Part B of this exercise.

For your convenience in duplicating, the following material is reprinted on page 168 of the tear-out section in the teacher's manual.

The True Jesus

A. *False Images.* In a classic work entitled *Your God Is Too Small*, the author writes of some false images people have of Jesus. Sometimes these false images make them reject Jesus. Listed below are several of these wrong-headed, non-biblical images of the Jesus. Comb through the New Testament and find a biblical quote that shows a more accurate image of Jesus.

Jesus, Meek and Mild: Jesus is depicted as excessively obedient, pious and effeminate. He looks like he walked off a holy card.

⟨Find an example from the gospels where Jesus is manly and strong.⟩

Jesus, Superman: In this image of Jesus his divinity is so emphasized that he comes out looking like Superman of the comics and movies. His divinity makes him seem unreal and totally separate from us.

⟨Find some examples of Jesus' humanity, his being "like us in everything but sin."⟩

Jesus, the Warm Fuzzy: Jesus is the heavenly security blanket. He's up on his heavenly shelf for you to pull down to help you cope with the tough times, to escape from the responsibilities of life. He's an escape hatch who'll make us feel good all over.

⟨Find some instances where Jesus challenges us to grow up, to become mature disciples.⟩

B. *Your Title for Jesus:* Imagine that Jesus came today in the flesh to preach his message again. He selects you to be one of his apostles and assigns you the job of being his advertising agent. Using images from the world of music, advertising, politics and the movies, list three titles that you would give to him. Explain what each of these reveals about him.

Title #1: _____ _____

Title #2: _____ _____

Title #3: _____ _____

3. You might wish to use the film *The Happy Prince* to discuss Oscar Wilde's image of Jesus. The story focuses on redemptive love.

Session 4: **Jesus of the Councils**

1. Present carefully the reasons why doctrines about Jesus had to develop.

2. In your discussion of the church being guided by the Holy Spirit, you might raise these questions:

- What is the value of having a final authority on disputed questions (for example, the Supreme Court, a parent, a baseball umpire, a football referee)?

- Could the Christian community have survived without official teachers to guide it? Explain.

- How do the pope and bishops protect Christian faith today? Can Christians believe whatever they want to believe and still be called Christian? Suppose, for example, a person does not hold to the divinity of Christ. Is this person a Christian? Explain.

3. Review the four major Christological controversies in the section "Jesus of the Councils." Use the outline entitled "What the Early Councils Teach about Jesus" as a structure for the notes you put on the board or the overhead.

4. You might ask students to review this material for homework and then briefly quiz them in the next class.

Session 5: **The Nicene Creed**

1. Recite the Nicene Creed together for your opening prayer.

2. Divide the students into three groups. Each group must prepare a short explanation of several lines of the creed. They may use the text and their own insights for the presentation.

3. Call on each group to explain its section of the Creed.

4. Work through the reflection entitled "The Many-Sided Jesus." Allow time for the journal exercise of composing their own creed. This could be completed as a homework assignment.

Session 6: **Contemporary Issues**

1. *The sisters and brothers of Jesus.* Students are interested in this question and much appreciate the Catholic answer to it.

   This issue often leads to the doctrine of Mary's perpetual virginity. You might discuss this and share with students the insight that Mary's life-long virginity was a sign of her exclusive dedication to God's will. It points to her special consecration to God for life. She who carried the Lord within her is special among us. Mary's virginity is a sign of Jesus' uniqueness.

   Perhaps this question will also lead to a discussion of the role of church tradition. As Catholics, we have a deep respect for tradition, both the process of handing on the faith and that which is handed on. Tradition includes scripture, dogmas, key doctrines of the church, the major writings and teachings of the church Fathers and the living and lived faith of Christians throughout the ages. To ignore tradition is to ignore the working of the Holy Spirit in the church. We must appreciate the essential role of tradition when reflecting on any Christological question. For help in presenting the topics of tradition and Mary's role in the church you might consult Chapter 24 of Richard McBrien's *Catholicism*.

2. *Who is responsible for Jesus' death?*

   A. We recommend that you show and discuss one of the fine audiovisuals annotated above.

   B. Carefully read and discuss the quotation from Vatican II provided in the text. Also present the argument that the opponents of Jesus who were immediately responsible for his death were "representative sinners" for all of us.

   C. Have students work the exercise "Love Your Enemy." Use the questions at the end to generate a discussion on prejudice in our own culture, especially the cancer of anti-Semitism.

Session 7: **Summary and Evaluation**

1. Choose seven students to read the summary statements. Ask them each to explain the statement they have read.

2. Review carefully the focus questions and have students respond to them in class. Clarify where needed.

3. You can use the following for the quiz.

For your convenience in duplicating, the following material is reprinted on page 169 of the tear-out section in the teacher's manual.

Quiz on Chapter 9

Name: _____

Date: _____

Matching: Match the title to the appropriate statement.

    A. Son of God
    B. Good Shepherd
    C. High Priest
    D. Lord
    E. King
    F. Suffering Servant
    G. Prophet

_____ 1. Refers to ruler or master; used as a translation for the word *Yahweh*

_____ 2. One who testifies to the truth

_____ 3. Refers to Jesus' dominion over the universe

_____ 4. Designates Jesus' true identity as the Second Person of the Trinity

_____ 5. Refers to Jesus as the mediator between God and his people

True (+) or False (0)

_____ 6. The Council of Nicea taught that Jesus has the same nature as God, that he is God.

_____ 7. The essential mistake of Docetism was that it emphasized Jesus' humanity so much that it neglected his divinity.

_____ 8. It is proper to call Mary the Mother of God.

_____ 9. According to Catholic tradition, Jesus' "brothers and sisters" were his blood brothers and sisters.

_____ 10. The creed we recite at Mass is the Lateran Creed.

_____ 11. It is proper to say that Jews today were responsible for Jesus' death.

_____ 12. The Council of Chalcedon taught that Jesus is both God and human.

_____ 13. Catholics believe that Jesus gave the power to teach to Peter and his successors.

_____ 14. Doctrine about Jesus developed to communicate the truth of the gospel to people of different cultural backgrounds.

_____ 15. The Chi-Rho is an anagram for the first letters of a short creed.

Answers:

1.	D	9.	false
2.	G	10.	false
3.	E	11.	false
4.	A	12.	true
5.	C	13.	true
6.	true	14.	true
7.	false	15.	false
8.	true		

Session 8: **Planning a Service Project**

1. Be sure to assign the final journal entry exercise at the end of the chapter.

2. Then, spend a period planning a mini-service project to be done during the next week. This would be a great way to conclude the Jesus course.

Adaptation for Parish Religious Education Classes

Step 1: **Introduction** (30 minutes)

1. Use the song "Emmanuel" by Amy Grant for opening prayer.

2. Explain the power and significance of titles in our culture. Use examples from Session 2 above.

3. Have the students brainstorm on the titles of Jesus. As they mention key titles from the chapter, explain their significance. Do the exercise "Faith in Symbol."

Step 2: **Conciliar Teaching on Jesus** (30 minutes)

1. Read through a missalette copy of the Nicene Creed (or use the version given in this chapter). Introduce your discussion of the creed by warning against the twin dangers of Docetism and Arianism.

2. Carefully analyze the creed line by line.

3. Recite the creed prayerfully at the end of the exercise.

Step 3: **A Contemporary Christological Question** (30 minutes)

1. Since time is limited, we suggest you take up the issue of anti-Semitism.

2. Read together and discuss this section of the chapter.

3. Assign and discuss thoroughly the exercise, "Love Your Enemy."

   Alternative: Show and discuss a film on anti-Semitism as annotated above.

chapter 10

Meeting the Risen Lord

▪ *introduction* ▪

From a religious formation point of view, this final chapter is the most important in the book. It takes up the issue of how a believer can meet and respond to the living Lord.

The chapter begins by looking at the role of faith in a believer's life and then turns to the various ways we can meet Jesus in the church. It discusses the Christian community and introduces the students to the saints as models of discipleship. Mary is seen as the best model of Christian holiness.

The sacraments, material signs of Christ's presence today, are reviewed, particularly the Eucharist as the central act of Christian worship and source of nourishment for Christians who want to follow Jesus.

The scriptures are discussed as a vital source of inspiration. The words and narratives in the gospels link us to the historical life of Jesus. In the scriptures we are called to friendship with Jesus. The chapter emphasizes the need to spend time with Jesus by praying, in order to further develop the relationship. Four traditional forms of prayer are given.

Finally, the chapter shows that we can meet Jesus through others. It points to the example of Christian heroes, but also reminds us that Jesus can be encountered in everyone we meet, especially "the least of these."

This chapter is more than a list of ways to meet Jesus Christ. We try to set a tone of invitation, emphasizing that Jesus wants to be our friend and wants to influence our lives and, through us, the lives of others.

We can never overemphasize the importance of our own personal witness as disciples and friends of Jesus in sharing this chapter's content with our students. Personal faith testimony on how the Lord works in our lives has the potential, God willing, to enliven the faith of our students. May the living Lord be with all of us as we invite our students to encounter him in prayer, in scripture, through the saints, in the Christian community, and in every person we meet.

Further Reading for the Teacher

Bernardin, Joseph Cardinal. *Christ Lives in Me: A Pastoral Reflection on Jesus and His Meaning for Christian Life*. Cincinnati, OH: St. Anthony Messenger Press, 1985.

> Some excellent reflections on Jesus. Chapter 3 on following Jesus offers several practical ways to follow in the footsteps of the Master.

The Christian Brothers. *Prayer Forms*. Mystic, CT: Twenty-Third Publications, 1987.

> This short work contains 22 prayer ideas for classroom use.

Cooke, Bernard. *Sacraments and Sacramentality*. Mystic, CT: Twenty-Third Publications, 1983.

> An outstanding introduction to the sacraments. It looks on marriage—the sacrament of friendship—as a key sacrament in a system of grace that stresses friendship.

Farrell, Edward. *Prayer Is a Hunger*. Denville, NJ: Dimension Books, 1972.

> Many have found this book an outstanding help in the prayer life. Your students will, too.

Guzie, Tad. *The Book of Sacramental Basics*. Mahwah, NJ: Paulist Press, 1982.

> An excellent, clear introduction to the sacraments.

Harrington, O. P. Wilfred. *The Prodigal Father*. Wilmington, DE: Michael Glazier, 1982.

> This outstanding work summarizes the Christian message.

Link, S. J., Mark. *Challenge*. Valencia, CA: Tabor Publishing, 1987.

> A very good meditation program based on *The Spiritual Exercises of St. Ignatius*. This is part of a three-book series which also includes *Decision* and *Journey*.

Lustiger, Cardinal Jean-Marie. *The Lord's Prayer*. Huntington, IN: Our Sunday Visitor, Inc., 1988.

> A thought-provoking, scripturally-based discussion of the Lord's Prayer and how it can help us grow.

Moore, Joseph. *A Teen's Guide to Ministry: You Can Make It Happen*. Liguori, MO: Liguori Publications, 1988.

> A practical and well-written guide to teen ministry. Your students can profit from this.

126

Pennington, O. C. S. O., Basil. *Challenges in Prayer*. Wilmington, DE: Michael Glazier, 1982.

A primer on prayer. Many helpful insights on getting started in the prayer life.

Shea, John. *The Challenge of Jesus*. Chicago, IL: Thomas More Press, 1984.

Powerful insights from a theologian who has made popular the notion of "theology of story."

Walsh, Michael, ed., *Butler's Lives of the Patron Saints*. San Francisco: Harper & Row, 1987.

A great reference book on the saints.

Suggested Audiovisual Ideas

Butterfly (27-minute, videocassette, Paulist Productions). A modern story of resurrection where faith provides hope in the aftermath of death.

The Eucharist (10-minute color film, Teleketics). A meditative film presenting the Eucharist through the symbols of our life poured out in service of others and the desire to be close to God.

Father Kolbe (17-minute, filmstrip-cassette, Don Bosco Multimedia). A great example of a modern-day saint who offered his life in place of a fellow prisoner in Auschwitz.

Gods of Metal (27-minute color film, Maryknoll Films). Depicts peacemaking as an obligation of every Christian. This outstanding work shows the effects of the arms race.

Hungers of the Human Family (15-minute color film, Dovco). Shows the various hungers of our times and turns to Jesus as the one who can satisfy them.

Meditative Series I,II, and III (a series of two-minute films, Ikonographics). Can be used for in-class prayer exercises.

The Needle's Eye (27-minute, videocassette, Paulist Productions). A good illustration of meeting our Lord in others. A medical student is challenged to live a life of service to the poor.

Our Christian Prayers (10-episode filmstrip series with cassettes, ROA). A review of the major ways Christians pray. Analyzes some key prayers, for example, the Our Father in episode 2.

The Peacemaker (seven-minute color film, Teleketics). Depicts a knight who is mortally wounded but forgives his enemy. Helps us see that we share in the Lord's work of peacemaking.

Prayer (a series of six filmstrips with records, ROA). Titles include: 1. To Pray Is To Live; 2. To Pray Is To Listen; 3. To Pray Is To Wait; 4. To Pray Is To Be Simple; 5. To Pray Is To Share; and 6. To Pray Is To Say Yes.

Prayer: Yesterday, Today, and Tomorrow (color filmstrip, Twenty-Third Publications). A brief and interesting introduction to Christian prayers.

The Selfish Giant (27-minute, 16mm-animated, ROA). Despite being a "children's" classic, this story illustrates our encounter with Christ in others.

Shine On! (13-minute color film, Mass Media Ministries). A modern parable of discipleship in which a wanderer receives the mark of Jesus. Shows that following Jesus demands that we pick up our crosses, but crosses lead to the joy of Easter.

Something Beautiful for God (50-minute color film, Time-Life). The television documentary on Mother Teresa and her work of love in India.

Who Are the Debolts? And Where Did They Get 19 Kids? (72-minute, 16mm, Mass Media Ministries). A great contemporary model of Christ in Christian community.

Work of Love (35-minute color film, Ikonographics). A powerful film of love. Shows the vision of Mother Teresa who sees our Christian response primarily in terms of response to the "least of these."

Objectives

That students . . .

1. *Consider* the challenge of Jesus to love everyone, especially the weak and defenseless.
2. *Realize* that Christian faith means a commitment to following the Lord Jesus Christ.
3. *Recognize* and *discuss* the various presences of Jesus in the world today.
4. *Characterize* the grace-filled invitations of the Lord in the sacraments of reconciliation and the Eucharist.
5. *Experience* praying as an important means to draw closer to the Lord.
6. *Appreciate* examples of Christian holiness.
7. *Reflect* deeply on their own vocation to holiness.
8. *Evaluate* their own personal commitment to Jesus Christ.
9. *Review* the main ideas of the book.

Time Used

Allow eight class days for this material. Add an additional day for a eucharistic service, and another for review.

Procedure

Session 1: **Introduction**

1. Begin by reciting the opening prayer to the chapter from Galatians. Ask the students for the significance of Paul using the word "Abba."
2. Listen to the song "That's What Faith Must Be" by Michael Card from his album *Present Reality*.

3. Introduce the students to the different presences of Jesus in this chapter: in themselves, the church, the saints, the sacraments, scripture, prayer and others.

4. Work together the exercise "Jesus and You" to reflect on Christ's presence in each of your students. Allow them some class time for the journal exercise.

Session 2: **Meeting Jesus in the Christian Community**

1. Discuss the three quotes in the section entitled "Jesus Lives in You." These quotes are:

St. Paul	on faith
St. Teresa of Avila	on Christian love
Anonymous	on personal responsibility

2. You might play for your students the song "Distressing Disguise" by Michael Card from his album *Present Reality*. This will tie in to the three quotations and stress "whatsoever you do to the least of my brothers and sisters, you do unto me."

3. Turn to the section entitled "Jesus Lives in the Church." Read together the passage from the *Dogmatic Constitution on the Church*. Stress that we Christians are a presence of Christ in the world.

4. The exercise entitled "list making" will help reinforce the points made above.

5. You might also want to use the following exercise to drive home these themes:

For your convenience in duplicating, the following material is reprinted on page 170 of the tear-out section in the teacher's manual.

Jesus and You

Study the following quotations. Discuss what each statement means. Do you think they accurately describe Jesus? Explain.

"He changed sunset into sunrise."—St. Clement of Alexandria

"The three greatest dolts in the world: Jesus Christ, Don Quixote and I." — attributed to Simon Bolivar (1783–1830)

"If Jesus Christ were to come today, people would not even crucify him. They would ask him to dinner, and hear what he has to say, and make fun of it." — Thomas Carlyle

Now apply each quotation to yourself and answer the following questions:

1. Have you ever changed sunset into sunrise? For example, when, if ever, have you brought hope to someone? When have you been light to others?

2. Would today's world consider you foolish for your Christian beliefs? Explain.

3. Have you ever defended a Christian belief and been ridiculed for doing so? Explain. Do you have any strong religious convictions that would be laughed at according to today's standards? If so, are you proud of them? Explain.

Session 3: **Meeting Jesus in the Saints**

1. Before this session begins, you might research some of your students' first names and write down any information about the saint they were named after. Do as many as you have time for. Present to them what you find out. Students have always appreciated the efforts we've taken in this fun exercise.

2. Read through the material in the section entitled "Saints." Emphasize Mary as the model of sainthood, a perfect symbol of one who was open to God's will. Encourage the students to read the lives of the saints as inspiration for living our vocation to discipleship.

3. Use the following exercise to further their own interest in saints. Perhaps students could do this in small groups. We recommend a trip to the library. They could use Catholic almanacs, books on the saints, catechisms and encyclopedias to collect this information. Set a time limit.

For your convenience in duplicating, the following material is reprinted on page 171 of the tear-out section in the teacher's manual.

Saints Test

See if you can identify the following patron saints.

The patron saint of . . .

EASY

1. carpenters
2. doctors
3. Ireland
4. United States
5. fishermen
6. throat infections
7. hopeless (desperate) causes

HARD (These will need some research.)

8. accountants
9. housewives
10. protection against abortion
11. motorways
12. France
13. television

14. music
15. theologians
16. teenagers (esp. girls)
17. missions
18. young workers
19. young students
20. scripture scholars

Answers:

1. Joseph, husband of Mary
2. Luke, the Evangelist
3. Patrick
4. Blessed Virgin Mary (Immaculate Conception)
5. Peter, the Apostle
6. Blaise
7. Jude, the Apostle
8. Matthew
9. Martha
10. Catherine of Sweden
11. John the Baptist
12. Mary, B.V.; Joan of Arc; Therese of Lisieux
13. Clare; Gabriel the Archangel
14. Cecilia
15. Thomas Aquinas
16. Maria Goretti
17. Francis Xavier
18. John Bosco
19. John Berchmans
20. Jerome

4. *Discussion Questions*:

   a. Which saint is your favorite? Why?
   b. Who today would you say is a "living saint?"
   c. Is sainthood always recognized?

Session 4: Meeting Jesus in the Sacraments

1. When covering the sacraments you might wish to make a chart to indicate the various ways Jesus is present to us sacramentally. For example:

SACRAMENT	JESUS IS PRESENT . . .
Baptism	as a companion on life's journey in a particular faith community
Confirmation	as a strong advocate sending his Spirit of love to enable us to become witnesses to the world with adult faith
Eucharist	as an intimate friend who shares life on a daily basis

Reconciliation	as a forgiving friend who heals guilt and alienation
Anointing of the Sick	as a healer in times of suffering
Matrimony	as a companion in marriage and family life
Holy Orders	as a minister to the Christian community

2. Allow the students to voice any negative feelings they have towards the sacraments and try to clarify any misunderstanding, especially regarding Mass and Eucharist.

3. We recommend that the students rate themselves in regards to Jesus, using the exercise entitled "Bread of Life."

4. *Strong Recommendation*:   As you wind down the course, we encourage you to prepare and celebrate a penance service and/or a eucharistic celebration with your students, especially if you have not done so earlier in the course. What better way to meet the living Lord than through a positive experience of these two sacraments?

    If you celebrate reconciliation, have the students prepare an examination of conscience. Use the categories of "Loving God," "Loving Neighbor" and "Loving Self."

    Your students could also prepare the eucharistic celebration. The following work sheet might help.

For your convenience in duplicating, the following material is reprinted on pages 172–173 of the tear-out section in the teacher's manual.

Eucharistic Planning Sheet

Planning committee:

Date: Time: Place:

Celebrant:

Homilist:

Mass Servers:

Eucharistic ministers:

Cantor and/or Music Group:

Commentator:

Banners/posters made by:

Audiovisuals selected by:

            set up by:

Decorations selected by:

            set up by:

Bread prepared by:

THE MASS

Music:

      Entrance

      Response after reading

      Presentation of the Gifts

      Acclamation

      Holy, Holy, Holy

      Lamb of God

      Communion

      Closing

Readings:

First Reading	read by:
Second Reading	read by:
Response	read by:
Gospel	read by: celebrant

Petitions offered by:

Presentation of the Gifts by:

Eucharistic Prayer:

Eucharistic Ministers:

Session 5: **Meeting Jesus in Scripture**

Note: Time has already been spent throughout the course on the gospel narratives and sayings of Jesus. There is no need to do here what has already been done. However, one exercise at this time might serve as a good review:

Exercise: Do one or more of the following.

a. For one extra credit point per quote, have students write down as many sayings of Jesus that they can from memory.

b. Select 50 or so quotes of Jesus. Divide the class into teams. Read the first part of the quote and have students complete it. Assign points for correct answers.

c. Have students comb through the gospels to come up with their five favorite sayings of Jesus. Allow each student to read one and give a short instruction on what this quote means to him or her.

Session 6: **Meeting Jesus in Prayer**

1. Begin class with an imaginative prayer meditation with the Lord. Darken the room. Light a candle. Take the students back to Jesus' historical days. Vividly describe a scene. Put yourself and students into it. Hear Jesus talking his words of love to you and your students. Let the scriptural word speak to your hearts.

2. Write the four forms of prayer on the board or overhead. Discuss the advantages of each form.

3. **Witness**: Describe how you pray, and talk about the value of prayer in your life.

4. Have the students work the exercise "Jesus on Prayer" and discuss their responses.

5. In covering this section, you might take a traditional prayer like the Our Father and analyze it line by line. Encourage your students to compose and share their own prayers. Finally, you might review the rosary here as a good prayer practice that focuses attention on the great Christian mysteries. If so, recite five decades.

Session 7: **Meeting Jesus in Others**

1. Begin with the following exercise:

For your convenience in duplicating, the following material is reprinted on page 174 of the tear-out section in the teacher's manual.

Heroes

1. Meet in five or six groups, each group making a list of heroes in various fields (for example, music, sports, politics, organized religion, science, movies). Share the list.

Discuss:

a. What qualities do the people you listed share in common?

b. What is a hero? Do we live in an age of heroes or anti-heroes? Explain.

c. Is it a good thing to have someone to admire? Why or why not?

2. Whom do you admire more than anyone else? Explain why. Share your personal hero with your classmates.

3. Heroes in the Christian community are known as saints. Here is a checklist of qualities acknowledged as traits of the true saint. Place a check mark in the first column to show the qualities your personal hero has. Then place an **X** next to the qualities that you yourself exhibit pretty often.

_____ _____ a. This person reveals the true meaning of life.

_____ _____ b. The Lord shines through this person.

_____ _____ c. This person lives the Christian life.

_____ _____ d. This person shows others how to be great.

_____ _____ e. This person does ordinary things in an extraordinary way.

_____ _____ f. We can meet the living Jesus in this person.

What would you add to this list?

Are there any "unsung heroes" in your life? If so, plan to show your admiration for them in some way.

2. Have students read the section "Jesus Lives in Others."

3. Select one of the following options:

a. Show an audiovisual that depicts a modern hero.

b. Invite to class a person who ministers to others; have this person speak on what motivates him or her to serve others.

c. Witness to a Christian hero in your life.

4. *Homework*:   Have students write a response to the following in their journal.

A friend of yours is not convinced that Jesus is alive and well and active in the world. How would you respond to your friend? List and then write an essay discussing at least five ways the Lord can be met today.

Session 8: **Conclusion**

1. To review the material covered in this book, use the following questions to test student knowledge of Jesus. You might also want to use this as a take-home test.

For your convenience in duplicating, the following material is reprinted on pages 175–176 of the tear-out section in the teacher's manual.

A Jesus Catechism

Here are some questions you should be able to answer about Jesus now that you have finished this book. If you are able to discuss these intelligently, you have grasped many of the major ideas you have studied.

1. What does the name Jesus mean and why is it appropriate that our Lord was given this name?

2. What can the Christian say in response to the charge that there was no historical Jesus?

3. Discuss how the gospels came to be, and tell something about each of them.

4. Explain the importance and significance of Jesus' use of *Abba, Amen*, his parables and his teaching on love.

5. Discuss some major events in the history of the Jews, and how these events may have contributed to the expectation of a messiah in Jesus' day.

6. Identify and briefly comment on the significance of Herod the Great, Pontius Pilate, Herod Antipas, the Pharisees, the Sadducees, the Essenes and the Zealots.

7. When was Jesus born? When did he die? What was the meaning of his birth?

8. List five miracles of Jesus and tell what each means.

9. What was the human Jesus like? You may wish to comment on some of the

following traits: his sensitivity, his friendship with others; his teaching ability; his genuineness. Who were his friends? Name the apostles.

10. What did Jesus teach? Can his message still mean something to people today? Explain. Is it meaningful to you? Explain.

11. Each of the gospel writers has his own unique portrait of Jesus. Briefly discuss how two of the gospels present Jesus. Use several examples from each to substantiate your discussion.

12. What is the meaning of the death of Jesus?

13. Why is the resurrection absolutely essential to our salvation and to our faith in Jesus?

14. What are some objections people have raised about the resurrection? How might we respond?

15. How can Christians live the paschal mystery in their daily lives?

16. Discuss the meaning and significance of each of the following New Testament titles of Jesus:

    a. Christ
    b. Suffering Servant
    c. Son of Man
    d. New Moses
    e. Son of God
    f. Lord
    g. Prophet, Priest and King

17. How does the risen Jesus meet us today? Explain.

18. Discuss two heresies concerning Jesus. How did the church respond to these heresies? What is the Nicene Creed?

19. Discuss several key doctrines about Jesus that have come down to us from the early councils. Be sure to mention the teaching of the Council of Chalcedon (451) and discuss its meaning.

20. What does it mean to believe in Jesus? If you wish to be his disciple, what must you do?

---

2. To reinforce the affective objectives of the course, use the following final essay question. Return these to the students and encourage them to save it and refer to it from time to time in the next few years to see how their beliefs have changed or been strengthened.

"Who Do You Say I Am?"

Write a 300-word essay responding to the following:

Who is Jesus and what does he mean to me?

3. You might want students to write responses to Jesus' questions in the conclusion of the book. These should be included in their journals.

4. Your students might also enjoy doing the character sketch of Jesus suggested in the final journal entry. Be sure to end the course with a reading of "Footprints." Students always like this one.

Adaptation for Parish Religious Education Classes

Step 1: **Introduction** (5 minutes)

Begin with the song "Distressing Disguise" by Michael Card from *Present Reality*. Discuss it if the students seem willing to do so. Alternately, read "Footprints" from the Prayer Reflection at the end of the chapter.

Step 2: **Ways of Meeting Jesus** (40 minutes)

1. Discuss the role of faith in following Jesus as outlined in the section "Jesus Lives in You."

2. Work the exercise "Jesus and You."

3. List on the board or overhead projector the following ways of meeting Jesus. Briefly explain each one:

- the church - Christian community
- the saints
- the sacraments (focus on the Eucharist)
- the scriptures
- prayer
- others (Christian heroes)

Step 3: **Conclusion** (40-50 minutes)

Use of one of the two review suggestions listed above (Session 8):

Cognitive review—The Jesus Catechism

Affective review—"Who Do You Say That I Am?"

Tear-Out
Section

138

One Solitary Life

Here is a young man who was born in an obscure village, the child of a peasant woman.

He worked in a carpenter shop until he was thirty.

He never wrote a book. He never held an office. He never owned a home. He never had a family. He never went to college.

He never did one of the things that usually accompany greatness. He had no credentials but himself.

While he was still a young man the tide of public opinion turned against him. His friends ran away. He was turned over to his enemies.... He was nailed to a cross between two thieves.

While he was dying, his executioners gambled for the only piece of property he had on earth, and that was his coat. When he was dead, he was laid in a borrowed grave through the pity of a friend.

Nineteen centuries have come and gone, and today he is . . . the leader of the column of progress. I am far within the mark when I say that all the armies that ever marched, and all the kings that ever reigned, have not affected the life of man upon this earth as has this One Solitary Life.

Relationship with Jesus. How are you doing in your relationship with Jesus? Judge your life with Jesus by writing your initials on the point on the dotted line which best represents where you are with him right now.

1. active .... passive

2. exciting .... dull

3. close .... distant

4. friendly .... stranger

5. deeply .... shallow
   personal   & cold

Discuss:

1. If Jesus were to appear to you, what one question would you like to ask him?

2. Share several of the questions you and your classmates would like to ask Jesus. Imagine how he might answer them. Decide where you might go to find additional information.

Jesus Pre-test

Fill in the blanks:

1. What does the name *Jesus* mean? _____

2. What was Jesus' profession? _____

3. Name several of his relatives: _____

4. Where was he born? When? _____

5. What might he have looked like? _____

6. How much formal religious education did he have? _____
   _____

7. What was his nationality? his religion? _____

8. Where did he live? _____

9. How old was he when he died? _____

10. Who were his best friends? _____

True or False

_____ 11. Jesus experienced temptation to do evil as we do.

_____ 12. From the time he was a child, Jesus knew everything there was to know because he was also God.

_____ 13. Jesus was like us in *all* things except sin.

_____ 14. While he was on earth, Jesus started the church with a pope and bishops, just like we have today.

_____ 15. The gospels were written when the apostles were with Jesus.

_____ 16. Jesus' main proclamation was "the kingdom of God."

_____ 17. Jesus got angry at certain things and people.

_____ 18. Sometimes Jesus didn't follow all the rules of the Jewish religion.

_____ 19. Because he was God, Jesus really didn't have to eat and sleep each day.

_____ 20. Jesus knew the exact future before it occurred because he was God.

140

Friend or Foe?

Name	Identify	For/against
1. Herod Antipas	_____	_____
2. John the Baptist	_____	_____
3. Caiaphas	_____	_____
4. Scribes	_____	_____
5. Gamaliel	_____	_____
6. Pharisees	_____	_____
7. the Magi	_____	_____
8. Herod the Great	_____	_____
9. Pontius Pilate	_____	_____

For further discussion, list some other people who have expressed opinions about Jesus and religion. Examples include:

Friedrich Nietzsche: argued that "God is dead"

Jean Vanier: sees Jesus in the mentally and physically disabled

Karl Marx: saw religion as the opiate of the people

Hugh Hefner: glorifies sexual indulgence

Mohandas Gandhi: greatly admired Jesus but could not understand lukewarm Christians

Quiz on Chapter 1

Name: _____

Date: _____

Multiple Choice: Choose the letter that best completes the statement.

_____ 1. The primary source of information about the existence of Jesus: (A) the Evangelists; (B) Pliny the Younger; (C) Suetonius; (D) Josephus.

_____ 2. This Jewish historian referred to Jesus in his historical writings: (A) Tacitus; (B) Suetonius; (C) Josephus; (D) Pliny the Younger.

_____ 3. The town where Jesus grew up: (A) Bethlehem; (B) Nazareth; (C) Jerusalem; (D) Samaria.

_____ 4. The image of Jesus that portrays him as a liberator: (A) Person for Others; (B) Way to Freedom; (C) Savior; (D) Human Face of God.

_____ 5. The person who gave a faith-filled response to Jesus' question "Who do you say that I am?" (A) Gamaliel; (B) Peter; (C) Caiaphas; (D) Mark.

_____ 6. The fifth Roman prefect in Judea: (A) John the Baptist; (B) Pontius Pilate; (C) Caiaphas; (D) Hillel.

_____ 7. This person might have been related to the Essenes' desert community; he was a precursor of the Messiah. (A) John the Baptist; (B) Pontius Pilate; (C) Caiaphas; (D) Peter.

_____ 8. The high priest of the Jerusalem Temple: (A) Josephus; (B) Thaddeus; (C) Caiaphas; (D) Joseph of Arimathea.

_____ 9. The "separated ones," who observed the Law strictly: (A) Sadducees; (B) Essenes; (C) Sanhedrin; (D) Pharisees.

_____ 10. The image of Jesus that stresses his example of true human living: (A) Way to Freedom; (B) Savior; (C) Human Face of God; (D) Person for Others.

Short Essay: At this stage of your life, who do you say that Jesus is?

Family Ties

Examine Matthew's genealogy carefully. You'll find there something almost unheard of in Jewish genealogies of Jesus' day—the names of *women*. These aren't just any women either, but well-known Old Testament characters whose reputations would make the reader think twice. What are they doing in Jesus' family tree? For example, there is Tamar, a Canaanite woman who donned the dress of a prostitute to seduce her father-in-law Judah and bear his son (Genesis 38). Or take Rahab, another prostitute. She hid Joshua's spies in Jericho, thus helping the Israelites conquer the Promised Land (Joshua 2). Ruth is a final example. She was a non-Jew, a Moabite, who followed the advice of Naomi and charmed the wealthy Boaz into marrying her.

To Jesus' contemporaries, these women were symbols of determination, quick-wittedness and faith. Yahweh showered his blessings on Gentiles, adopted them into the family of his Chosen People and used them to fulfill his promises.

Assignment: All of us should study our family trees to learn about the fascinating people who are part of our own story. Construct your own family tree as far back as you can. Be sure to interview grandparents and great-grandparents to find out some of the interesting details in the story of your family. Please share with your classmates at least three new things you discovered about your family heritage.

Journal: Write a two-page biography of a significant woman in your life—your mother or one of your grandmothers. Discuss three of her best qualities. Report how you are like her or different from her. Write about what she means to you.

What's in a Name?

A person's name helps root that person in history. It says "Here is a real person with this set of parents, with this occupation, from this place." Every Christian name carries some significance. For example, here are some common biblical names with their meanings:

David — beloved of God

Ann — full of grace

Michael — he who is like God

John — God is gracious

Ruth — a beautiful friend

Joseph — let God add

Using a book on names as a reference, research the meaning of your first and middle name:

Name: _____ **Meaning**: _____

Name: _____ **Meaning**: _____

If you bear the name of a Christian saint, prepare a brief report on his or her life. If you are not named after a Christian saint, report on the life of your favorite saint. *The New Catholic Encyclopedia*, *Butler's Lives of the Saints* or some other book on the saints should be of help. Share your research in a report to the class.

Challenge: Find the meaning of your surname. Perhaps your parents or grand-parents would know what it means. Your public library should have books on last names you can use for reference. Does your surname tell you about an ancestral profession, place of residence, a physical attribute or first name of an ancestor? Does this help to give you a sense of identity and pride in your family?

Map Exercise

Locate the following places on a map of the Holy Land. Then, read the references given below. In the space provided, mention how the particular locale figured in Jesus' ministry.

Cana (John 2:1–12) _____

_____

Capernaum (Matthew 4:12–17) _____

_____

Jordan River (John 1:19–34) _____

_____

Emmaus (Luke 24:13–35) _____

_____

Bethany (Matthew 26:6-13) _____

_____

_____

Using a good bible atlas (for example, *The Macmillan Bible Atlas*), find a map of Jerusalem in Jesus' day. Use it to outline the Temple and indicate the various places of interest during the last week of Jesus' life.

Crossword Puzzle Clues

1. Temple
2. Herod the Great
3. Egypt
4. gold
5. incense
6. myrrh
7. Bethlehem
8. star
9. stable
10. shepherds
11. Jesus
12. Nazareth
13. Incarnation
14. Annunciation
15. Virgin Birth

A. the great building project of Herod the Great

B. cruel king who slaughtered the Innocents in Bethlehem

C. place of sanctuary for Joseph, Mary and the baby Jesus

D. a gift of the magi: worthy of a king

E. a gift of the magi: burnt offering to God

F. a gift of the magi: an ointment used to prepare a body for burial

G. Joseph's ancestral hometown

H. the sign to the magi of Jesus' birth

I. location of Jesus' birth

J. the common witnesses to Jesus' birth

K. name that means "Yahweh is salvation"

L. Jesus' hometown in the province of Galilee

M. "God becoming human in Jesus"

N. the angel Gabriel appearing to Mary

O. Mary conceiving and bearing Jesus by the power of the Holy Spirit

How Many of These Can You Do in 30 Minutes?

1. The name Jesus means _____.

2. Two points learned from the virginal conception: _____

_____

3. Jesus' hometown is _____.

4. Jesus was probably born in _____ ⟨place⟩.

5. Luke traces Jesus' genealogy to _____.

6. Nazareth is located in the province of _____.

7. _____ is a Jewish rite where a 13-year old becomes a "son of the Law."

8. Jesus probably studied the _____ like other 5-year-old boys.

9. The _____ was a place of Jewish assembly an worship.

10. Two words of Aramaic that Jesus spoke: _____.

11. In Matthew, God's protection of his Son is symbolized by the flight to ___

_____

12. Both _____ and _____ recognized Jesus as the Messiah during Jesus' presentation in the Temple.

13. The term meaning God becoming man in Jesus is _____.

14. The angel _____ visits Mary in Luke's gospel.

15. The word *bar* means _____ in the phrase "Jesus bar Mary."

16. The English equivalent of the Greek word meaning "Messiah" or "Anointed One" is _____.

17. The title _____, from Isaiah, means "God is with us."

18. *Jesus* is a late form of the Hebrew name _____.

19. The Jews believed that the Messiah would come from _____'s descendants.

20. Bethlehem is in the province of _____.

21. The gifts of _____, _____, and _____, are symbols used in Matthew's infancy narrative.

22. The ruthless king of Judea, _____, was a volatile mixture of policy and passion.

23. Psalm _____ refers to three kings honoring the Messiah.

24. The Emperor at the time of Jesus' birth was _____.

25. Matthew was primarily writing to a _____-Christian audience.

26. Luke was primarily writing to a _____-Christian audience.

27. The gospel infancy narratives are more _____ than historical.

28. Jesus' genealogy reveals two important truths: Jesus is both

_____ and _____.

Quiz on Chapter 3

Name: _____

Date: _____

Identify the twelve apostles.

_____ 1. I am a fisherman and Peter's brother.

_____ 2. I am also known as Thaddeus.

_____ 3. I am a former revolutionary.

_____ 4. I am a fisherman whom Jesus called the "rock" of the new church.

_____ 5. I was a tax collector before my conversion.

_____ 6. I did not believe until I saw the risen Christ.

_____ 7. I am known in history as "the younger" or "the lesser."

_____ 8. I am also called Nathaniel.

_____ 9. I am the "beloved disciple" and a "son of thunder."

_____ 10. I asked Jesus to show us the Father; my name means "lover of horses."

_____ 11. I am the other "son of thunder."

_____ 12. I betrayed Jesus and committed the sin of despair.

Short Fill-in: Give an example of each of the following types of miracles.

_____ 13. raising from the dead

_____ 14. an exorcism

_____ 15. a nature miracle

_____ 16. a physical healing

Matching:

_____ 17. the precursor of Jesus who baptized the repentant

_____ 18. former high priest

_____ 19. high priest at Jesus' trial

_____ 20. wife of Herod Antipas

A. Herodias

B. Caiaphas

C. John the Baptist

D. Simeon

E. Herod Antipas

F. Annas

Your Religious Heritage

Parents' Names: _____

Interviewer's Name: _____

1. What faith did you choose to raise me in? Why?

   _____

   _____

2. When did you achieve a mature faith? (Note specific circumstances, if any.)

   _____

   _____

   _____

3. Who was the greatest influence on your religious growth?

   _____

   _____

4. What do you see as the greatest enemy to *my* faith? Why?

   _____

   _____

   _____

5. How important is Jesus in your life? Explain.

   _____

   _____

   _____

   _____

The Story of God's People at a Glance

c.1900 B.C.	The Patriarchs Abraham
1250 B.C.	Exodus: Moses and Joshua
1200–931 B.C.	Judges to Solomon *Golden Age:* King David (1010–970) Solomon (970–931)
931–721 B.C.	Divided Kingdom Samaria Falls (721)
721–587 B.C.	Kingdom of Judah Ends Exile: 587–538
587–333 B.C.	The Persian Period
333–63 B.C.	The Hellenistic Period Maccabees: 168–37
63 B.C.–A.D. 135	Roman Rule
6 B.C.	Jesus' birth
A.D. 30	Jesus' death
A.D. 45–48	Paul's Missionary Journeys
A.D. 50–100	New Testament Composed 66–70: First Jewish Revolt

God Protects His People

If we were to line up the oppressors of the Jews throughout the Old Testament, they would include the following:

- Egyptians
- Canaanites
- Assyrians
- Babylonians
- Persians
- Greeks
- Ptolemies (the Egyptians)
- Seleucids (the Syrians)
- Romans

Discuss:

1. Explain how the Jews might have survived in the midst of all these turmoils.

2. What is the primary nature of God's convenant promise to the Jews? (Is it self-rule? survival? a sense of identity? etc.)

Quiz on Chapter 4

Name: _____

Date: _____

Identify the group that best relates to the statement.

Pharisees
Sadducees
Essenes
Romans
Zealots

_____ 1. They hated the Romans.

_____ 2. They recognized only the Torah as inspired by God.

_____ 3. They believed in angels.

_____ 4. They accepted the doctrine of the resurrection of the body.

_____ 5. They cooperated with the Romans while being caretakers of the Temple.

_____ 6. They were closer to the beliefs of Jesus than any other of his day.

_____ 7. They were a strict monastic community in the desert.

_____ 8. John the Baptist may have been one of them.

_____ 9. They forced high taxes and harsh rules on the Jewish people.

_____ 10. They wanted the Messiah to lead a political kingdom.

_____ 11. Much knowledge about them has come through the discovery of the Dead Sea Scrolls.

_____ 12. They used crucifixion as a death penalty for slaves.

_____ 13. They advocated a religious holy war led by the Messiah.

_____ 14. They desired to live the Law (Torah) as perfectly as they could.

_____ 15. They placed a procurator (governor) in charge of Judea.

The Lord's Prayer—An Analysis

Read through the following imaginary parallel to the Lord's Prayer based on *Jewish sources*:

> Our Father, who art in Heaven. Hallowed be Thine exalted Name in the world which Thou didst create according to Thy will. May Thy Kingdom and Thy lordship come speedily, and be acknowledged by all the world, that Thy Name be praised in all eternity. May Thy will be done in Heaven, and also on earth give tranquillity of spirit to those that fear thee, yet in all things do what seemeth good to Thee. Let us enjoy the bread daily apportioned to us. Forgive us, our Father, for we have sinned; forgive also all who have done us injury; even as we also forgive all. And lead us not into temptation, but keep us far from all evil. For thine is the greatness and the power and the dominion, the victory and the majesty, yea all in Heaven and on earth. Thine is the Kingdom, and Thou art Lord of all beings forever. Amen.

The Lord's Prayer (cf. Luke 11:2–4)

> Father,
> Hallowed by thy name. Thy Kingdom come.
> Give us each day our daily bread;
> and forgive us our sins,
>   for we ourselves forgive
>   everyone who is indebted to us;
> and lead us not into temptation.

List any *differences* that you can identify between the two prayers:

1. _____

2. _____

3. _____

> For the person who can pray the prayer of Jesus, in a very real sense the kingdom has already come.

> —taken from *The New Testament: An Introduction* by Norman Perrin

Salvation Themes

The cleverness of many contemporary ad agencies is their use of the religious theme of salvation as a key appeal in selling their products. Hair-coloring products, for example, promise "salvation" from old age. This claim, of course, is false. No one and nothing can keep us from growing older—even though we might like to think so.

What do the following products promise in the way of "salvation?" Criticize the ads in light of Jesus' teaching.

Ad	*Salvation Theme*
soft drink	_____
beer	_____
aspirin or other pain reliever	_____
automobiles	_____
jeans	_____
underarm deodorant	_____

Optional: Make a tape of some commercials (audio or video) or find examples in printed media that use religious language to sell the product, for example, "have faith in," "trust in," "miracle," etc. Discuss how the advertiser tries to manipulate the buyer into purchasing the product.

154

Be a Good Samaritan (Please read Luke 10:29–37)

Jesus requires all of us to be Good Samaritans, to love even our enemies. This most popular of all parables has often been turned into an allegory through Christian history. Here is a popular interpretation of the parable.

Parable Elements	Allegorical Meaning	Your Interpretation
traveler	Adam (representing all humanity)	
Jerusalem	the heavenly city	
Jericho	the fallen world	
robbers	demons who strip Adam of immortality	
priest	Law	
Levite	prophets	
Samaritan	Jesus Christ (who heals humanity with oil and wine—comfort and admonition)	
inn	the church	
innkeeper	apostles: Peter and Paul	
Samaritan's return	second coming of Christ	

As a class, come up with your own allegory. Who are the victims of violence in *your* world? Who fails to take notice? What kind of aid can *you* and your classmates give? What would correspond to the inn?

Look at this parable in a creative way, interpret it in a modern-day setting, and then devise a service project where you and your classmates would actually give aid to a person who is hurting. Here are some examples: at an old folks' home; a hunger center; students in need of tutoring; etc. *Be a Good Samaritan!*

Excerpted from Jesus: Friend and Savior Teacher's Manual, by Michael Pennock. Copyright © 1990 by Ave Maria Press, Notre Dame, IN 46556. Permission to reprint granted for classroom use in the context of this course.

Quiz on Chapter 5

Name: _____

Date: _____

Part 1: Here is a summary of Jesus' message. Briefly explain what Jesus meant by each point.

1. Reign of God

2. Forgiveness

3. Abba

4. Salvation

5. Love and Judgment

6. Rejoice

Part 2: Select, read and briefly discuss the meaning of any three of Jesus' parables. Then explain how each parable teaches about God's reign.

The gospel according to _____.

Part 1:   Examine the following sources and consider their importance for your gospel.

Sources:

A. Beatitudes (Sermon on the Mount)

B. Passion Narrative

C. Old Testament Prophecies

D. Healing Miracle Stories

E. Parables

F. Resurrection Accounts

G. Lord's Prayer

H. Reign of God Sayings

I. Proverbs

J. Infancy Narratives

K. Nature Miracle Stories

L. The Golden Rule

M. Jesus' Baptism and Temptation in the Desert

N. Jesus' Entry into Jerusalem

O. The Transfiguration

Part 2:   Choose any 10 of the 15 sources that you consider are the most important. List them in your order of priority.

1: ____	6: ____
2: ____	7: ____
3: ____	8: ____
4: ____	9: ____
5: ____	10: ____

Gospel Search

Place an X to indicate if a particular gospel takes up the theme or event listed.

	MT	MK	LK	JN	ALL	NONE
Birth of Jesus						
Slaughter of the Innocents						
Stable and Manger						
The Annunciation						
Baptism of Jesus by John						
Temptation in the Desert						
Wedding Feast at Cana						
Beatitudes						
Parable of the Prodigal Son						
Peter's Commission						
Parable of the Good Samaritan						
Lord's Prayer						
Transfiguration						
Raising of Lazarus						
Jesus Enters Jerusalem						
The Last Supper						
The Passion						
Veronica Wipes Jesus' Face						
Jesus Falls Three Times						
Two Criminals Crucified						
Resurrection of Jesus						
Disciples on the Road to Emmaus						
Great Commission						
The Ascension						

Excerpted from Jesus: Friend and Savior Teacher's Manual, by Michael Pennock. Copyright © 1990 by Ave Maria Press, Notre Dame, IN 46556. Permission to reprint granted for classroom use in the context of this course.

Quiz on Chapter 6

Name: _____

Date: _____

Part 1: *Match* each quotation below with one of the scriptural images of Jesus from Chapter 6 of the text.

A — The Servant Messiah (Mark)

B — The New Moses (Matthew)

C — Savior of the World (Luke)

D — The Word of God (John)

_____ 1. "My mother and my brothers are those who hear the word of God and put it into practice."

_____ 2. "I am the true vine, and my Father is the vinedresser."

_____ 3. "Then he looked angrily round at them, grieved to find them so obstinate. . . ."

_____ 4. "This was done to fulfill what the prophet had spoken."

_____ 5. "You are Peter, and upon this rock I will build my church."

_____ 6. "I tell you, there is rejoicing among the angels of God over one repentant sinner."

_____ 7. "He could work no miracle there because of their lack of faith."

_____ 8. "I am the good shepherd."

_____ 9. "Father forgive them; they do not know what they are doing. . . .This day, you will be with me in paradise."

_____ 10. Jesus went up to the mountainside and began to instruct them. "How blessed are the poor in spirit: the kingdom of Heaven is theirs."

Part 2:

List the three stages of gospel formation:

Stage 1: _____

Stage 2: _____

Stage 3: _____

Define the following terms:

kerygma: _____

_____

synoptic: _____

_____

Jesus the Person

What kind of person was Jesus? We can learn something of what a person is by what a person does, or doesn't do.

Jesus was . . .

1. **a lay person**: *not* a consecrated religious leader.
2. **a common person**: *not* a professional theologian or philosopher.
3. **a reformer**: *not* a revolutionary.
4. **someone who enjoyed life**: *not* an ascetic.

   (He ate and drank and accepted dinner invitations from the rich and poor alike.)

Jesus . . .

5. **preached the reign of God**: he was a teacher.
6. **lived God's will**: he went against some customs and laws, for example certain fasting and Sabbath regulations.
7. **spoke like a prophet**: he didn't worry about what people said or thought of him.
8. **identified himself with**:

   despised persons
   minorities
   heretics
   prostitutes
   adulterous people
   women
   political collaborators
   tax collectors
   lepers
   children

9. **lived his own words**: "Love your enemies."

   (Adapted from Hans Kung's, *On Being A Christian*.)

The Face of Jesus

Jesus Christ is the most famous person who ever lived, yet we have no picture or painting of his real likeness. The Jewish religion of Jesus' day forbade personal portraits for fear of *idolatry*, the worshipping of false images. Nor do the gospels give us a physical description of Jesus. We simply don't know for certain if he was short or tall, plain-looking or handsome, dark or fair-skinned.

After several generations, Christians did begin to portray our Lord. The catacombs of Rome contain the earliest images of Jesus. There he appears as a curly-haired young man similar to young King David. At other times he appears as a bearded man with long hair, the style worn by pious Jewish men of Jesus' own day. Other early wall paintings show Jesus as the Good Shepherd, holding a lamb across his shoulders. Where Rome did tolerate Christian communities, Jesus appears as a teacher and a miracle-worker, his two main vocations described in the gospels. And after Constantine recognized Christianity, Jesus was increasingly shown as a heavenly king crowned in glory.

The early church Father, St. Jerome, concluded that some of God's majesty must have shown through Jesus' human body. He wrote:

> Had he not had something heavenly in his face and his eyes, the apostles never would have followed him at once, nor would those who came to arrest him have fallen to the ground (quoted in Denis Thomas, *The Face of Christ*, New York: Doubleday, 1979, p. 17).

Christian artists of later centuries largely adopted St. Jerome's view. Although a true representation of Jesus can never be captured, artists decided that paintings and statues of Jesus should be compatible with the beauty of the mystery of God becoming flesh. Jesus is *God*-made-man.

Only after about the year 1000 did paintings of Jesus as a suffering, crucified Savior become widespread. Depiction of a crucified Jesus appeared first in Byzantine art and then spread to the West. By the time of the Renaissance, artists increasingly portrayed a human Jesus. Rembrandt, for example, chose Jewish men from his city of Amsterdam as his models for Jesus. His paintings are excellent, classic representations. They portray a real man like us.

In the 19th century cheap, "syrupy" paintings of Jesus began to appear. Perhaps you have seen some of these. In them we see a delicate, "wimpy," soft-featured, almost effeminate Jesus. Missing is the strength that drove the money changers out of the Temple. Certainly, Jesus was no unassertive waxen image.

However we picture Jesus, we must consider three facts:

- He was a Jew who spent many hours on the road outdoors in the sun. He was surely tan, rugged, strong and chiseled by the elements. Traveling up and down the roads of Palestine took fierce drive and commitment.

- Jesus was a carpenter. He was a workingman with calloused hands. It takes strength and skill to hoist up cross beams, to cut timber and to work wood into useful implements.

- Jesus attracted all kinds of people. Strong, rough fishermen dropped their nets to follow him. The rich invited him to dinner. The poor, the sick and children longed for his touch. Women followed him around and cared for his needs. All types of people wanted to be his friend. There had to be something incredibly attractive about this Jesus of Nazareth.

Honesty and You

Honesty is the touchstone of a person's character. It determines how genuine and authentic he or she really is. How do you measure up? How honest are you?

Answer the following questions as honestly as possible. Assume in all cases that you won't get caught.

	yes	no	?
1. Would you ever take a set of towels or an ashtray from a motel room in which you were staying?	___	___	___
2. If you found a wallet with $10 and the owner's identification, would you keep the money?	___	___	___
3. Would you ever lie about your work experience in filling out an application?	___	___	___
4. If your employer misfigured your hours and credited you with four hours you didn't work, would you not mention it and keep the money?	___	___	___
5. Would you make up a story to tell your parents rather than take your punishment for coming home late?	___	___	___
6. While pulling out of a tight spot in the shopping center, you dent the car parked next to you. You know it will cost a couple of hundred dollars to have it fixed. Furthermore, if you report the accident, your insurance rate will skyrocket. Would you leave without reporting the accident?	___	___	___
7. Would you cheat on a college entrance exam?	___	___	___
8. If a teacher praised you for your original, creative ideas on a topic when in fact you were just repeating what someone else had said in another class, would you let the teacher continue to think the ideas were your own?	___	___	___

Reflection: For a person of true integrity, "getting caught" is not an issue. Would you change any of your answers if the instructions above read: "Assume that what you do will become public knowledge." What does this say about your level of integrity?

164

Quiz on Chapter 7

Reflect on the following qualities of Jesus:

1. friendship
2. strength and gentleness
3. honesty and courage
4. treatment of women

In a well-written essay, give specific examples of how Jesus lived out these qualities. Use some of the insights from Chapter 7 to develop your argument. Make certain that your essay is coherent and organized. Perhaps developing a brief outline first may help.

Dateline Jerusalem

Imagine that you and your classmates are staff members of the *Jerusalem Gazette*. You are to produce a Saturday morning edition reporting the crucifixion of Jesus and the events leading up to it.

Sample Story Ideas:

1. *Obituary* for Jesus of Nazareth

2. *News stories* summarizing the events of Holy Week

3. *In-depth interviews*:

■ *with Jewish and Roman officials*: members of the Sanhedrin, Pontius Pilate, Pilate's wife, Herod, the Roman centurion at the site of the crucifixion, etc.

■ *with Jesus' friends*: Mary, Peter, John, Joseph of Arimathea, Lazarus and the like

■ *with Judas* (you might also report his death)

■ *with Jesus' mother*

4. *Background features*: the Roman law of occupation and capital punishment, the workings of the Sanhedrin, the method of crucifixion, burial practices in Palestine

5. *Weather report*

6. *Editorials*: one supporting Jesus' condemnation and one opposing it

7. *Letters to the Editor*: from the mother of the "good" thief, Barabbas, Simon of Cyrene and others

8. *An account of the Last Supper* given by an apostle, perhaps Thomas

Let your imagination suggest other story ideas. Perhaps some students could do line drawings of the arrest, trial and crucifixion. Others could devise ads and be responsible for the layout and design of the paper.

Attitude Toward Death

Christian belief in a personal resurrection through Jesus Christ should affect your attitude toward death. React to the following statements.

    5 — strongly agree
    4 — agree
    3 — don't know
    2 — disagree
    1 — strongly disagree

_____ 1. I'd like at least 24 hours to prepare for my death.

_____ 2. I'd like to know how I am going to die.

_____ 3. It is foolish to worry about death.

_____ 4. It is wrong to fear death.

_____ 5. I feel uneasy around dying people.

_____ 6. Death leads to resurrection.

_____ 7. How I live will make a difference when I die and meet my judgment.

_____ 8. Those who believe in Jesus will be raised on the last day.

Share and discuss your responses.

Heaven.   Complete these open-ended sentences.

1. When I see the Lord in the afterlife, I will thank him for . . .

2. When I see the Lord in the afterlife, I will ask him . . .

3. A famous person I would like to see in heaven is . . .

4. The person I want to spend eternity with is . . .

5. Heaven will be like . . .

6. Belief in my personal resurrection . . .

Optional: Share your responses and discuss the attitudes that they reveal.

Research: Choose one of the following religions or cults and research its beliefs about the afterlife:

■ Aztec or Incan religion

■ Hinduism, Buddhism, or Islam

■ Judaism

■ Christianity

■ a modern cult

■ ancient Roman or Greek religion

Report your findings to the class.

Heaven and Hell

Answer these questions in complete paragraphs. Do you agree or disagree with the following positions? Why or why not?

1. Heaven is an eternal state but we don't know what it is physically like.

2. There is a hell and people are in it.

3. Life will continue forever after death for those who live like Jesus commanded.

4. Hell is annihilation—the total discontinuation of life and existence.

5. Heaven is a possibility for everyone.

6. Heaven and Hell begin here, and continue in the afterlife.

7. Not everyone will receive eternal life, because God determined all before you were born.

The True Jesus

A. *False Images.* In a classic work entitled *Your God Is Too Small*, the author writes of some false images people have of Jesus. Sometimes these false images make them reject Jesus. Listed below are several of these wrong-headed, non-biblical images of the Jesus. Comb through the New Testament and find a biblical quote that shows a more accurate image of Jesus.

Jesus, Meek and Mild: Jesus is depicted as excessively obedient, pious and effeminate. He looks like he walked off a holy card.

⟨Find an example from the gospels where Jesus is manly and strong.⟩

Jesus, Superman: In this image of Jesus his divinity is so emphasized that he comes out looking like Superman of the comics and movies. His divinity makes him seem unreal and totally separate from us.

⟨Find some examples of Jesus' humanity, his being "like us in everything but sin."⟩

Jesus, the Warm Fuzzy: Jesus is the heavenly security blanket. He's up on his heavenly shelf for you to pull down to help you cope with the tough times, to escape from the responsibilities of life. He's an escape hatch who'll make us feel good all over.

⟨Find some instances where Jesus challenges us to grow up, to become mature disciples.⟩

B. *Your Title for Jesus:* Imagine that Jesus came today in the flesh to preach his message again. He selects you to be one of his apostles and assigns you the job of being his advertising agent. Using images from the world of music, advertising, politics and the movies, list three titles that you would give to him. Explain what each of these reveals about him.

Title #1: _____   _____

Title #2: _____   _____

Title #3: _____   _____

Quiz on Chapter 9

Name: _____

Date: _____

Matching: Match the title to the appropriate statement.

    A. Son of God

    B. Good Shepherd

    C. High Priest

    D. Lord

    E. King

    F. Suffering Servant

    G. Prophet

_____ 1. Refers to ruler or master; used as a translation for the word *Yahweh*

_____ 2. One who testifies to the truth

_____ 3. Refers to Jesus' dominion over the universe

_____ 4. Designates Jesus' true identity as the Second Person of the Trinity

_____ 5. Refers to Jesus as the mediator between God and his people

True (+) or False (0)

_____ 6. The Council of Nicea taught that Jesus has the name nature as God, that he is God.

_____ 7. The essential mistake of Docetism was that it emphasized Jesus' humanity so much that it neglected his divinity.

_____ 8. It is proper to call Mary the Mother of God.

_____ 9. According to Catholic tradition, Jesus' "brothers and sisters" were his blood brothers and sisters.

_____ 10. The creed we recite at Mass is the Lateran Creed.

_____ 11. It is proper to say that Jews today were responsible for Jesus' death.

_____ 12. The Council of Chalcedon taught that Jesus is both God and human.

_____ 13. Catholics believe that Jesus gave the power to teach to Peter and his successors.

_____ 14. Doctrine about Jesus developed to communicate the truth of the gospel to people of different cultural backgrounds.

_____ 15. The Chi-Rho is an anagram for the first letters of a short creed.

Jesus and You

Study the following quotations. Discuss what each statement means. Do you think they accurately describe Jesus? Explain.

"He changed sunset into sunrise."—St. Clement of Alexandria

"The three greatest dolts in the world: Jesus Christ, Don Quixote and I." — attributed to Simon Bolivar (1783-1830)

"If Jesus Christ were to come today, people would not even crucify him. They would ask him to dinner, and hear what he has to say, and make fun of it." — Thomas Carlyle

Now apply each quotation to yourself and answer the following questions:

1. Have you ever changed sunset into sunrise? For example, when, if ever, have you brought hope to someone? When have you been light to others?

2. Would today's world consider you foolish for your Christian beliefs? Explain.

3. Have you ever defended a Christian belief and been ridiculed for doing so? Explain. Do you have any strong religious convictions that would be laughed at according to today's standards? If so, are you proud of them? Explain.

Saints Test

See if you can identify the following patron saints.

The patron saint of . . .

EASY

1. carpenters

2. doctors

3. Ireland

4. United States

5. fishermen

6. throat infections

7. hopeless (desperate) causes

HARD (These will need some research.)

8. accountants

9. housewives

10. protection against abortion

11. motorways

12. France

13. television

14. music

15. theologians

16. teenagers (esp. girls)

17. missions

18. young workers

19. young students

20. scripture scholars

Eucharistic Planning Sheet

Planning committee:

Date: Time: Place:

Celebrant:

Homilist:

Mass Servers:

Eucharistic ministers:

Cantor and/or Music Group:

Commentator:

Banners/posters made by:

Audiovisuals selected by:
            set up by:

Decorations selected by:
            set up by:

Bread prepared by:

THE MASS

Music:

Entrance

Response after reading

Presentation of the Gifts

Acclamation

Holy, Holy, Holy

Lamb of God

Communion

Closing

Readings:

First Reading	read by:
Second Reading	read by:
Response	read by:
Gospel	read by: celebrant

Petitions offered by:

Presentation of the Gifts by:

Eucharistic Prayer:

Eucharistic Ministers:

Heroes

1. Meet in five or six groups, each group making a list of heroes in various fields (for example, music, sports, politics, organized religion, science, movies). Share the list.

Discuss:

a. What qualities do the people you listed share in common?

b. What is a hero? Do we live in an age of heroes or anti-heroes? Explain.

c. Is it a good thing to have someone to admire? Why or why not?

2. Whom do you admire more than anyone else? Explain why. Share your personal hero with your classmates.

3. Heroes in the Christian community are known as saints. Here is a checklist of qualities acknowledged as traits of the true saint. Place a check mark in the first column to show the qualities your personal hero has. Then place an **X** next to the qualities that you yourself exhibit pretty often.

_____ _____ a. This person reveals the true meaning of life.

_____ _____ b. The Lord shines through this person.

_____ _____ c. This person lives the Christian life.

_____ _____ d. This person shows others how to be great.

_____ _____ e. This person does ordinary things in an extraordinary way.

_____ _____ f. We can meet the living Jesus in this person.

What would you add to this list?

Are there any "unsung heroes" in your life? If so, plan to show your admiration for them in some way.

A Jesus Catechism

Here are some questions you should be able to answer about Jesus now that you have finished this book. If you are able to discuss these intelligently, you have grasped many of the major ideas you have studied.

1. What does the name Jesus mean and why is it appropriate that our Lord was given this name?

2. What can the Christian say in response to the charge that there was no historical Jesus?

3. Discuss how the gospels came to be, and tell something about each of them.

4. Explain the importance and significance of Jesus' use of *Abba, Amen*, his parables and his teaching on love.

5. Discuss some major events in the history of the Jews, and how these events may have contributed to the expectation of a messiah in Jesus' day.

6. Identify and briefly comment on the significance of Herod the Great, Pontius Pilate, Herod Antipas, the Pharisees, the Sadducees, the Essenes and the Zealots.

7. When was Jesus born? When did he die? What was the meaning of his birth?

8. List five miracles of Jesus and tell what each means.

9. What was the human Jesus like? You may wish to comment on some of the following traits: his sensitivity, his friendship with others; his teaching ability; his genuineness. Who were his friends? Name the apostles.

10. What did Jesus teach? Can his message still mean something to people today? Explain. Is it meaningful to you? Explain.

11. Each of the gospel writers has his own unique portrait of Jesus. Briefly discuss how two of the gospels present Jesus. Use several examples from each to substantiate your discussion.

12. What is the meaning of the death of Jesus?

13. Why is the resurrection absolutely essential to our salvation and to our faith in Jesus?

14. What are some objections people have raised about the resurrection? How might we respond?

15. How can Christians live the paschal mystery in their daily lives?

176

16. Discuss the meaning and significance of each of the following New Testament titles of Jesus:

    a. Christ
    b. Suffering Servant
    c. Son of Man
    d. New Moses
    e. Son of God
    f. Lord
    g. Prophet, Priest and King

17. How does the risen Jesus meet us today? Explain.

18. Discuss two heresies concerning Jesus. How did the church respond to these heresies? What is the Nicene Creed?

19. Discuss several key doctrines about Jesus that have come down to us from the early councils. Be sure to mention the teaching of the Council of Chalcedon (451) and discuss its meaning.

20. What does it mean to believe in Jesus? If you wish to be his disciple, what must you do?